The Book of Girls' Activity Fun

ARCTURUS

ARCTURUS

This edition published in 2012 by Arcturus Publishing Limited
26/27 Bickels Yard, 151–153 Bermondsey Street,
London SE1 3HA

ISBN: 978-1-84858-391-7
CH002161EN

Written by Lisa Miles
Designed by Ariadne Ward
Additional text by Xanna Eve Chown
Illustrated by Robyn Neild
Edited by Kate Overy

Printed in Singapore

Supplier 16, Date 0412, Print Run 1621

Contents

There are hundreds of things to do inside this book - fun puzzles, cool quizzes, drawing ideas, things to make and MORE! Follow the girls on a fab adventure and check it out...

CRAFT ACTIVITIES
Don't forget to ask an adult for help with scissors!

Meet the girls!

The girls are going on an adventure!
Find out who's in the gang...

JESS

You can rely on Jess to be in charge! She's confident, musical and definitely the leader of the gang when it comes to an adventure!

Mini file

Loves: showing off!
Top skill: having great ideas
Always saying: Let's just do it!

Mini file

Loves: fashion and make-up
Top skill: designing cool outfits
Always saying: Looking good, girls!

ROXY

When it comes to style, Roxy is your girl! She knows just what to wear to create the right impression – and she always gives good advice to her friends!

ANNA

Anna is the girl who gets things done – and she's always sunny and cheerful. If her friends ever need a helping hand, she's the one to sort things out!

Mini file

Loves: surfing and being outdoors
Top skill: organising her friends
Always saying: We'll work it out!

CARLA

Helping animals is Carla's favourite hobby, and her pets are as important to her as her best friends. Oh, and she's a pretty good singer, too!

Mini file

Loves: all kinds of animals
Top skill: singing out loud
Always saying: Animals are people, too!

MILLY

Milly is good at being creative, from art and cookery to writing and singing. She loves making up stories, poems, rhymes and songs!

Mini file

Loves: making food for her friends
Top skill: inventing great lyrics
Always saying: Let's eat!

TAYLOR

Taylor is musical too, and she really knows how to move! Dancing is one of her favourite hobbies and she loves to teach her friends.

Mini file

Loves: music and dancing
Top skill: playing the guitar
Always saying: Wow, we rock!

Festival time

Jess and her best friends are going to a cool music festival. Unscramble Jess's secret message to find out what she wants to do first!

Hint: Try reading it in a mirror!

I WANT TO SEE MY FAVOURITE BAND!

Jess and the Go Girls

PART 1

The girls are off on an adventure! Big sisters Eve and Sadie are taking them to a music festival – which gives Jess an idea...

Jess fished around in her bag and produced a bunch of purple rubber wristbands. "Here we go!" she said as she handed them all out. The girls were in the queue for their local music festival and excitement was running high. They were wearing their best summer outfits – and carrying their wellies just in case it rained! The show was going on all afternoon and evening, and they were even being allowed to camp out for the whole night!

"This is going to be such an adventure!' Anna laughed excitedly.

"Thanks for bringing us," Roxy grinned at her big sister Eve and at Carla's big sister Sadie. "We promise to be good..." she continued in a pretend baby voice. Eve pulled a funny face and squeezed her little sister in a bear hug. "You'd better be! Otherwise all the parents will be chasing after me."

"We'll put up the tent straightaway and that can be our base camp," Sadie decided. The girls squealed in excitement as the queue began to move. They couldn't wait for the festival to begin!

As soon as their camp was ready, the girls set off. There was so much to see and do that it was hard to know where to go first. There were food stalls, clothes stalls, entertainers, buskers, bands, face painting and hair braiding. How could they fit it all in? Jess had a plan.

"There's a band playing that I REALLY want to see," she pleaded. "They're called Star Rock. They're so cool!"

"OK," Sadie said. "They're on in about an hour. Let's grab a snack then make our way over to the stage."

A short while later, the girls were at the front of the crowd and the atmosphere was buzzing. Star Rock ran on stage and instantly hit the audience with the sound of their jangling guitars and thudding drum beats.

"Wow!" yelled Jess above the noise. "These girls are incredible!" And as she watched, she began to have an idea...

What's Jess's big idea – and will the girls go for it? Continued on page 26

Puzzle parade

Which two pictures of Jess are exactly the same?

1 2 3 4 5

How quickly can you count the flowery wellies in this picture? Go for it!

Complete the grid so that every row, column and square has a white tent, a black tent, a grey tent and a spotty tent.

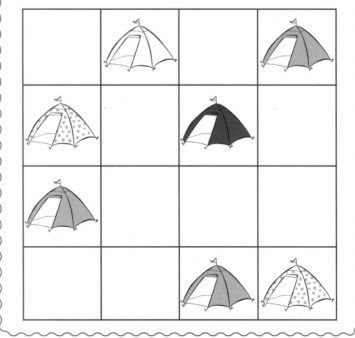

Wellie doodle!

What kind of wellies would YOU like to wear? Doodle them!

Are they stripy?

Are they flowery?

Are they bright and jazzy?

Spot the difference

There are ten tricky differences between these two pictures of the girls watching Star Rock. Ring them when you've found them!

What's your festival ID?

Read these questions and circle your answers. Then find out what kind of artist YOU would be at a festival!

 1 Your school art folder is full of:

A. sketches of rock stars
B. colourful drawings of your friends
C. fairytale creatures in forests

4 Your best birthday present is:

A. a karaoke DVD
B. a magic set
C. a make-up case

 2 At Christmas, you love:

A. going carol singing
B. jokes in Christmas crackers
C. making Christmas cards for your friends and family

5 Your bedroom wall is covered in:

A. posters of your favourite bands
B. posters of top movie stars
C. posters of cute animals

3 For a school play, would you rather:

A. plan the music
B. write the script
C. design the scenery

6 You're always getting told off for:

A. singing too loudly
B. doing dangerous tricks on your bike
C. making a mess with glue and paint

Read your results!

Mostly As
SOULFUL SINGER
You've always wanted to sing, so get up on that stage and give it all you've got!

Mostly Bs
CIRCUS TRICKSTER
You love making people laugh, so get out the juggling balls and tell those jokes!

Mostly Cs
FACE PAINTER
You're very creative and love art, so you'd be great at painting faces for fun!

Festival fun!

Jess is at the festival but she has lost her tent! Go round the campsite until you find it.

start

finish

Café

Face Painting

Puzzle parade

Which two tents are exactly the same?

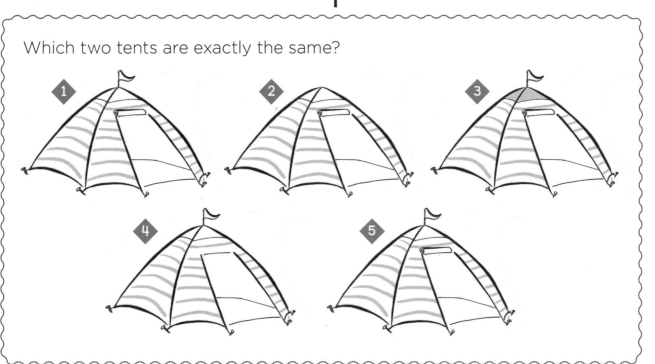

How many butterflies can you see in this picture?

Word mix up

The words below are all mixed up.
Unscramble them to find six fun
things to do at a festival.

SILNET OT SUMCI

_____ __ _____

TAE DOFO

___ _____

OG PAMNICG

__ _____

TEME NEIRDFS

_____ _____

ACEDN

_____

VEHA NUF

____ ___

Draw Jess!

Copy Jess's picture into the grid, square by square.

Snack time!

The girls are hungry and looking for a snack.
Help Jess and Milly find their way around the festival.
But beware – they can't go just anywhere!

Help Jess

Jess is on her way to the milkshake bar.
She mustn't pass any cupcake stalls,
but she can go past the drinks.

Help Milly

Milly is on her way to the sandwich bar.
She mustn't pass the drink stalls but
she can go past the cupcakes.

Drink
stall

Cupcake
stall

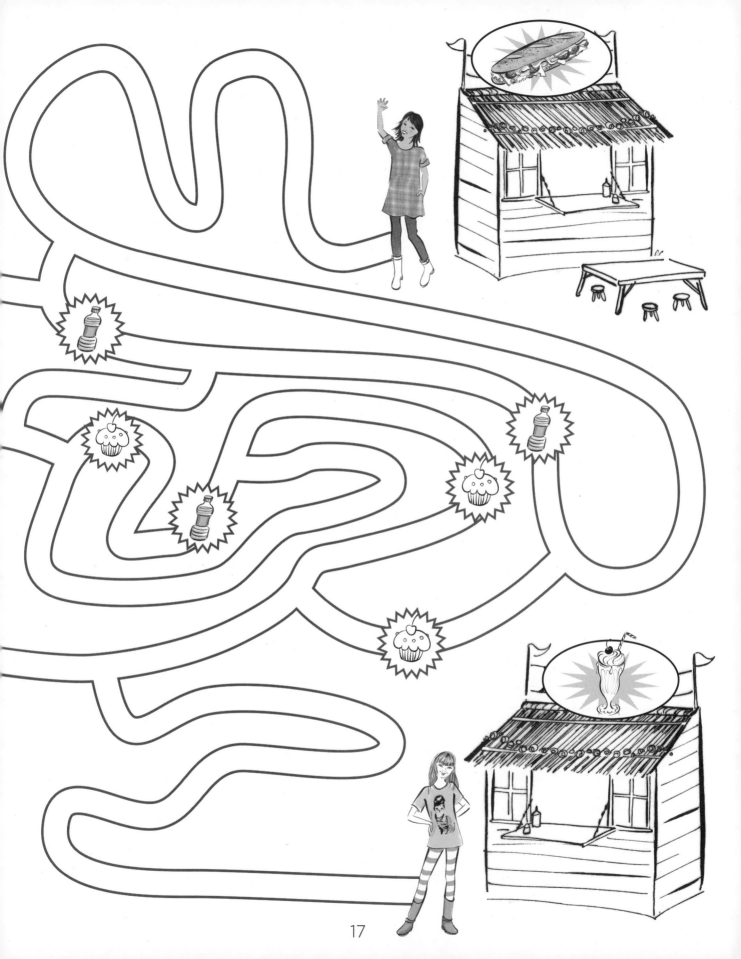

Musical words

Find the musical words in the grid. Look up, down, backwards, across and diagonally.

B	S	R	H	Y	T	H	M	H	E	T	K
K	A	H	I	T	K	M	E	N	U	R	H
Y	I	N	U	C	P	R	L	L	H	Z	F
O	M	N	D	T	K	E	O	L	H	H	P
N	E	Y	R	E	T	U	D	Y	G	U	K
G	I	K	U	N	G	R	Y	R	K	H	O
N	N	H	M	N	B	O	E	I	H	E	V
O	G	N	S	I	K	S	L	C	V	K	A
S	I	N	G	E	R	E	Y	S	N	C	N
A	I	G	U	I	T	A	R	H	U	O	G
D	B	O	D	S	I	L	T	O	N	R	C
F	S	R	S	C	I	T	E	S	S	A	B

Puzzle parade

How many words can you make out of the letters in the word FESTIVALS?

....

....

....

....

....

....

....

1-5
See if you can find a few more!

6-10
You're pretty good at this! Well done.

11-14
Wow! Celebrate in true festival style!

Which guitar is the odd one out?

Jess's challenge

People need entertaining at a festival. Take Jess's challenge and learn how to juggle!

TIP
If you're left-handed you'll find it easier to swap hands, so use your left hand where it says right and vice-versa!

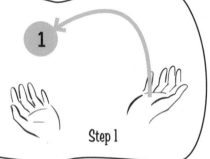

You will need

* Three juggling balls or three objects the same weight, such as small oranges

One ball...
Pass one ball back and forth between your two hands. Throw the ball up to eye level when you are confident you can catch!

Step 1

Two balls...
Now hold a ball in each hand. Throw the ball in your left hand to your right hand. Just before you are about to catch it, throw the other ball into your left hand. Keep practising and see if you can throw the balls up to eye level.

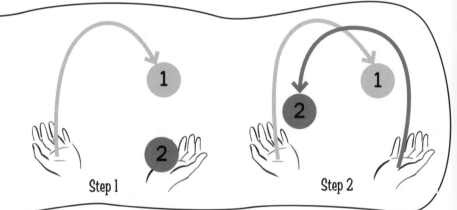

Step 1

Step 2

And three balls!
Now for the hard bit! Take two balls in your left hand and one in your right. Throw one ball from your left hand into your right one. As before, throw the right one back, but this time also throw the remaining ball in your left hand to your right! Yay!

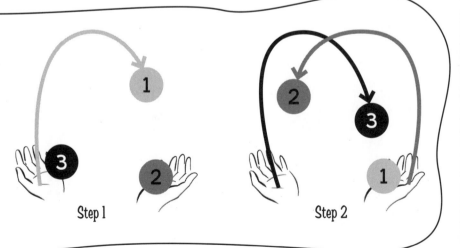

Step 1

Step 2

Design Jess's outfit

Design an outfit for Jess. What would she love to wear the most to a festival?

Give her some funky jewellery!

What shoes would she wear?

Fill it in!

What favourite accessory would Jess take on a weekend away?

....

21

Paint a butterfly face

Join in the festival fun and paint your friends' faces! There are loads of great patterns to try, but here's one to start you off.

You will need

* ✱ Face paints in colours of your choice. For this design, try white, pink, silver and black
* ✱ Face glitter, if desired
* ✱ Pink lipstick
* ✱ Make-up sponges
* ✱ Make-up brush
* ✱ Water to wet the sponges

 1 Using a damp sponge, cover the whole face with white paint to give a light, even colour.

2 Sponge a butterfly wing from one edge of the brow, right across the eyelid and down the cheek in pink paint. Then do this for the other eye, so that they match.

 3 On the outer edges of each wing, add a bold silver outline.

4 Load black paint onto your brush. Draw a butterfly body along the slope of the nose. Draw a head and antennae on the forehead. Then outline the wings in flourishing strokes.

5 Finish off with pink lipstick and a touch of glitter on each cheek!

Now ask a friend to paint your face!

Puzzle parade

There's a break in the music, so Jess is buying lunch.
Work out how much money she needs.

MENU

Hot dogs   £2.50
Sandwiches   £2.00
Apple   £0.60
Orange   £0.70
Chocolate bar   £0.50
Bottled drinks £1.00

∗ Jess wants two hot dogs! She's really hungry...
∗ Anna wants a sandwich and an orange
∗ Milly wants a sandwich and a chocolate bar
∗ Roxy wants a hot dog and an apple
∗ Taylor only wants a sandwich
∗ Carla wants the same as Milly
∗ All the girls want a drink

Write the
answer here

Jess needs: ....

Which tent flag doesn't have a pair?

1 2 3
4 5 6 7
8 9 10 11

10 things to do... for a festival!

Why not organise your very own mini-festival with your friends? Here's how to get going...

1. Where's the venue?

Do you or one of your friends have a great back garden or even an empty garage that you can take over for an afternoon? Remember to ask a grown-up first before you start organising!

2. The concept

Get together with your buddies and brainstorm everything that you think you might want at your mini-festival. Draw a map of your venue and plan out where everything is going to go.

3. Music on the menu

Which one of your friends is the music lover? Put someone in charge of the music and ask them to put together a playlist for your approval. Even better, does anyone play an instrument? Ask them to get a band together!

4. Liven it up!

Look around your venue. How can you make it look like a festival is happening here? You could hang flags and bunting from fences or trees, or if you are indoors put up some party decorations.

5. The entertainment

Are any of your friends budding entertainers? Do they tell jokes or do circus tricks? Book them to mingle with the crowd and provide the entertainment. Organise a few games and activities as well.

6. Refresh your guests

Think of some snacks and drinks that will be quick to serve and easy to eat – and won't make too much mess! How about wraps, cookies and bottled juice or water?

7. Chill out zone

Create a quiet area where your friends can go to chat and chill out. Camping chairs, hay bales or beanbags are all great for relaxing on.

8. Name your festival

Every festival has to have a name! Think of something catchy that represents you and your friends, or maybe the venue.

9. Don't forget the wristbands

No festival is complete without wristbands. You can use thick, coloured elastic bands or buy coloured ribbon, cut it into lengths and tie it into bands.

10. Promote your event!

Draw up a timetable of events, so that you know what's happening when and where. Then make sure that all your friends know about your mini-festival and all the fun things that are happening. Make flyers and hand them out!

Shopping spree

Roxy takes the girls shopping to get some cool outfits. Unscramble her message to find out where she wants to start!

Hint:
In each word, one letter is out of place!

GISRL, ET'SL OG OT HTE JICUE ARB FITRS!

Jess and the Go Girls

The festival is over, but the girls are still buzzing from the excitement. And Jess explains her idea... with a little help from Roxy.

PART 2

The girls plonked themselves down in Roxy's bedroom to discuss the festival. They'd had the best time ever, and there was so much for them to talk about.

"What was your favourite bit?" Anna asked the others.

"Mine was the toffee apples!" Milly grinned. "They were SO delicious!"

"Mine was getting my hair braided," Carla said. "I loved the big beads all down the front!"

"Mine was watching the street dance. I hope I'll be able to dance like that one day!" sighed Taylor.

"You already can, silly!" laughed Anna. "What about you, Jess?"

Jess smiled. "Well, Roxy and I have been talking. And we decided that the best bit was watching Star Rock – six cool girls who love to perform.... Who did they remind you of?"

There was a short silence – then Anna got the idea straight away. "You mean... US?"

"Yes!" exclaimed Jess. "Let's form our own band! Carla's a great singer and Taylor can dance AND play guitar. Milly can play keyboards and I've always wanted to play the drums. Roxy is desperate to be our stylist – she's already got our image worked out. And Anna, you're the organised one – you can be our band manager."

The girls looked at each other and knew it made sense. "OK let's do it!" Anna said decisively. "What next?"

Roxy hugged her knees, bubbling with excitement. "Let's go shopping. I've got some great outfits to show you. We are going to look SO cool".

"And I've even got a name," Jess added. "What do you think about Jess and the Go Girls?"

"Uh – excuse me," said Milly. "Why not Milly and the Go Girls?"

"Or Carla and the Go Girls?" added Carla.

"Maybe we should just be The Go Girls," said Anna, with a smile.

"OK," said Jess, reluctantly. Then she grinned.

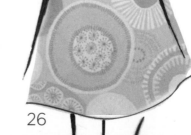

What will the girls do next? Continued on page 50

26

Design doodle!

Roxy loves rings! Doodle a
cool one here...

Does
it have
bling?!

Is it
junk
or jewels?

Is it cute or
completely
crazy?

Spot the difference

There are ten tricky differences between these two pictures of Taylor and Roxy trying on clothes. Ring them when you've found them!

How girly are you?

Read these questions and circle your answers.
Check the panel to find out how many points you scored
and find out about your girly side!

1 It's time for a new outfit. What do you choose?

A. a long, floaty dress in the latest fashion
B. a cool skirt and top
C. jeans – you can't beat them

2 Your new party dress is...

A. black because it never goes out of fashion
B. pink with a splash of black
C. pink – just pink all the way!

3 You join a new dance club. Your fave session is...

A. street dance in your top and jeans
B. classical ballet in tights and a tutu
C. modern dance and tap in a purple leotard

4 Your favourite read would be...

A. an adventure story about wild horses
B. a love story about a prince and princess
C. a spy story about a girl who saves the world

5 If you changed your first name, you would pick...

A. Danni
B. Felicity
C. Aurelia

Add up your points:

1. **A =** 3 points **B =** 2 points **C =** 1 point
2. **A =** 1 point **B =** 2 points **C =** 3 points
3. **A =** 1 point **B =** 3 points **C =** 2 points
4. **A =** 2 points **B =** 3 points **C =** 1 point
5. **A =** 1 point **B =** 3 points **C =** 2 points

5-8 points

TOMBOY

You do have a girly side, but you're a bit of a tomboy at the same time. That's cool!

9-11 points

GIRL POWER

You don't feel the need to be girly all the time. You can be a little bit sassy, too!

12-15 points

Girly Girl

Everything you do is girly and you just love being in the pink. Good for you!

Market maze

Roxy wants to buy something that no one else is wearing! Follow Roxy's trail through the vintage market in this order: jewellery, hats, shoes and dresses. But don't go past any handbags!

start

end

Puzzle parade

Which shadow exactly matches Roxy on a shopping trip?

Which two purses are exactly the same?

Complete the grid so that every row, column and mini-grid has one of each type of hairband inside it.

Precious word!

Move around this jewel and spell out the name of Roxy's favourite precious stone. Start at the arrow and move one space at a time in any direction. You must finish at the letter in the centre of the jewel.

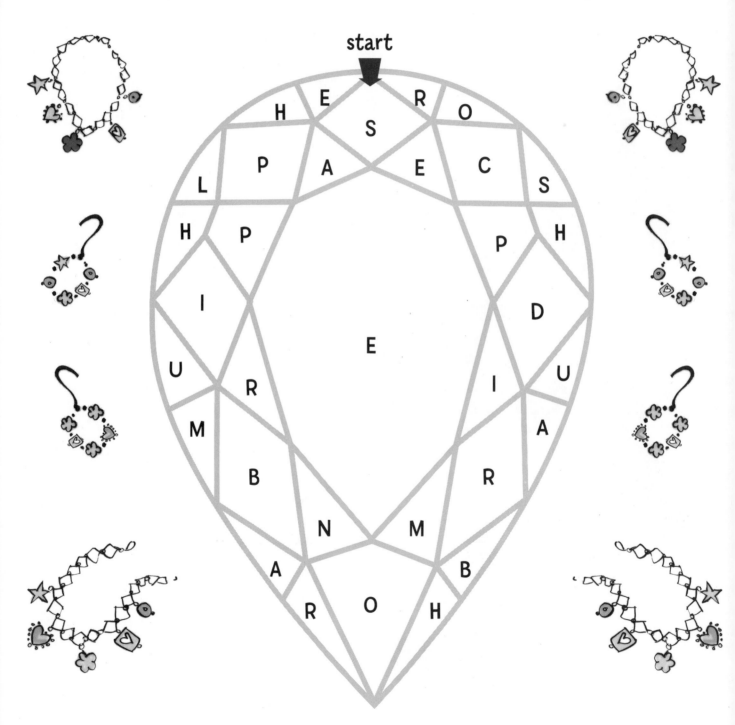

start

Draw Roxy!

Copy Roxy's picture into the grid, square by square.

Which band member are you?

Answer the questions and follow the arrows to find out what YOU would be if you were in a band, just like the girls!

start

Is it your dream to be centre stage?
— no
— yes

Fancy strutting in some big high heels?
— no
— yay

Do you get the party going?
— always
— not really

Are you more of a background person?
— maybe
— no

Can you rock the crowd?
— a little
— a lot

Are you super-organised?
— nope
— that's me

Ever been told you're a pretty good singer?
— yes
— maybe not

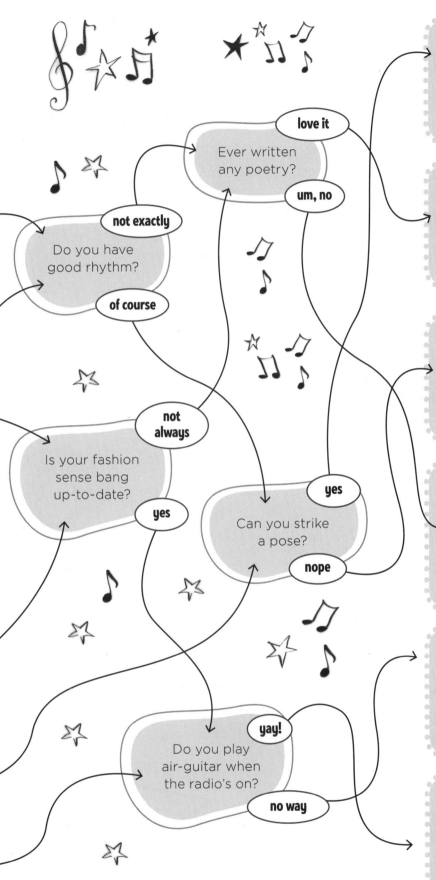

LEAD SINGER
You're the girl with the voice, just like Carla. Go for the lead!

SONGWRITER
You'll play the keyboard and write the songs, just like Milly!

DRUMMER
You've got the beat. Follow Jess and bang those drums!

BAND MANAGER
You're the organised one, just like Anna. So you're in charge!

BAND STYLIST
You've got style just like Roxy. The band's image is up to you!

GUITARIST
Pick up that guitar and start strumming. You rock, just like Taylor!

Ever written any poetry?
love it
um, no

Do you have good rhythm?
not exactly
of course

Is your fashion sense bang up-to-date?
not always
yes

Can you strike a pose?
yes
nope

Do you play air-guitar when the radio's on?
yay!
no way

Roxy's challenge

Look inside the depths of Roxy's handbag...
then challenge your friends to a game.

How to play

Give your friend one minute to look at this page. Then take the book away and ask her to write down as many items as she can remember that came out of Roxy's handbag. Now ask your other friends to do the same. Who can remember the most items?

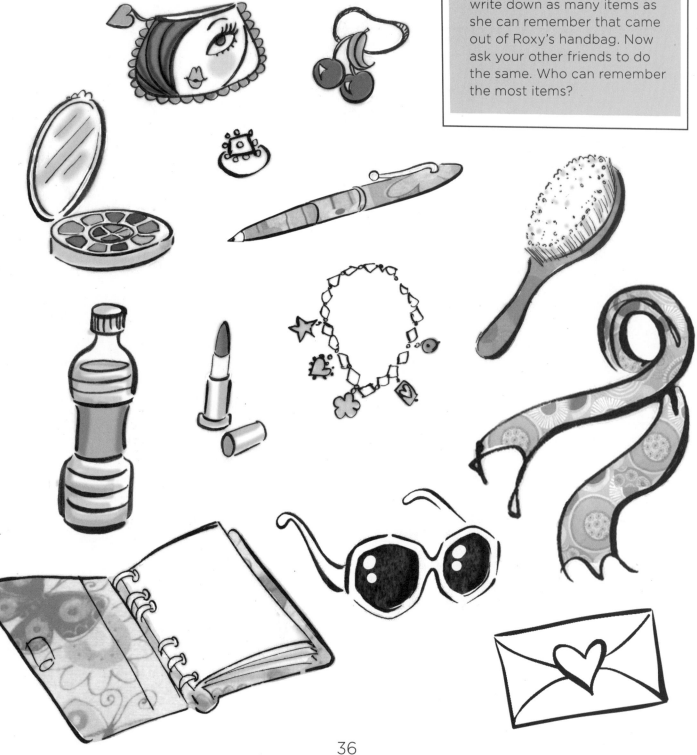

36

Pretty sudoku

Fill in the cute symbols to finish this sudoku!
One of each of the six pictures must appear in
each row, column and mini-box.

Puzzle parade

How many girl's names can you think of beginning with the letter R? Write them here!

Roxy

Roxy is looking for a comfy – but stylish – pair of pumps. Help her find them.

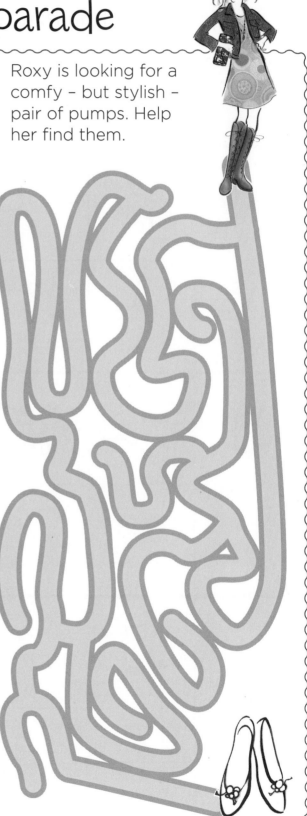

Doodle caboodle!

Roxy's dressing table is a whole caboodle
of fashion bits and bobs. Doodle them!

Organise
your
jewellery!

Hang up
your hat!

Parade
your
perfumes!

Puzzle parade

Cross out all the letters that appear twice, then rearrange the letters to find out what Roxy's favourite thirst-quencher is!

B S U B A R I J S K C K E A R

Write the answer here

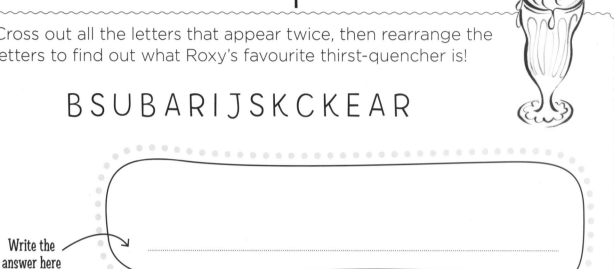

There are five differences between these two pictures of Roxy. Find them!

Find the message

Find Roxy's hidden message. Begin at the shaded square and trace a path through the letters to spell out words. You can go up, down and across, but not diagonally.

I	A	M	G	O	K	E	B	H	O	S	E
L	M	G	O	I	P	N	H	L	U	R	H
Y	O	R	O	N	G	T	T	O	H	P	F
O	S	G	I	N	L	O	S	S	O	H	P
N	E	A	L	A	T	S	T	T	S	O	A
B	A	K	I	S	A	T	A	E	I	F	A
C	L	A	B	L	K	A	N	R	H	H	N
U	L	K	I	N	I	R	A	A	V	H	I
S	S	I	O	L	N	A	R	O	C	K	B
A	D	N	O	S	D	T	A	O	U	B	L
D	Z	A	D	M	S	A	N	I	J	A	N
H	S	R	S	C	A	N	I	M	S	N	D

end

Write the message here:

___ ___ _____ _____ ___

_____ ___ _____ _____

Shop till you drop!

It's bargain time at the shops! Who will get to the best buy first?

How to play

For two or more players: Place counters, such as charms or small coins, on the start. Take it in turns to pick a number from the number chooser. Move your counter along the squares, according to the number you picked. Follow any instructions you land on.

For one player: See how many goes it takes you to get to the end!

Start

You're hungry already. Stop for a snack.

Miss a go.

Go back to check out a new shoe shop.

Go back 1 space.

You nip across town by bus, rather than walk.

Go forward 3 spaces.

Disaster - you forgot your purse!

Go back to the start.

Stop and chat to Jess.

Miss a go.

I rock!

Look in the mirror and see
yourself as a rock star! Doodle it....

Design Roxy's outfit

Design a festival outfit for Roxy! What would she love?

Does she look good in a hat?

What colour scheme suits her best?

Fill it in!

List four items that YOU would wear to a festival!

Puzzle parade

Follow the trail to find out which is Roxy's perfect accessory.

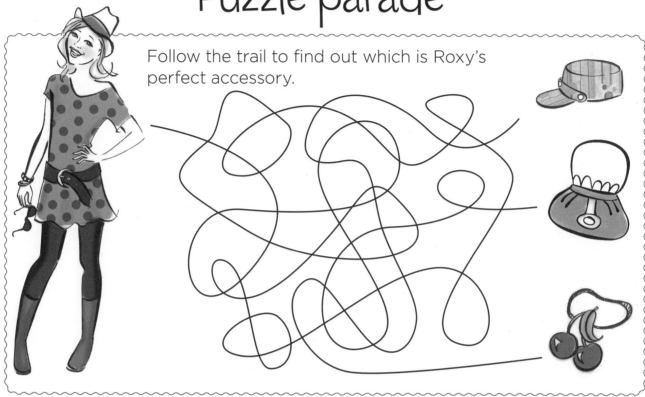

Circle the words that CAN'T be made out of the words WINDOW SHOPPING.

POSH   SWISH   WISHES   SHOE   NEW   NOW   WOOSH   SHINE   SHINDIG

Look at picture 1 of Roxy's bag. What's different in picture 2?

Glam up your flip-flops!

Give some plain flip-flops a bit of glamour – and you'll have an original pair of summer sandals that no one else has!

You will need

* Paper and pencil
* Plain flip-flops
* Decorations, such as sequins, plastic jewels, plastic flowers, feathers or coloured buttons
* Craft glue

 1 With your paper and pencil, sketch a design for your flip-flops. Do you want fluffy feathers, sparkly sequins or a bit of everything?

 2 Following your design, start in the centre and carefully stick your decorations down one strap.

 3 Repeat for the other strap, following the same pattern (or maybe not, if you want to go asymetrical!).

Now your 'new' flip-flops are ready to wear. Your feet look fabulous!

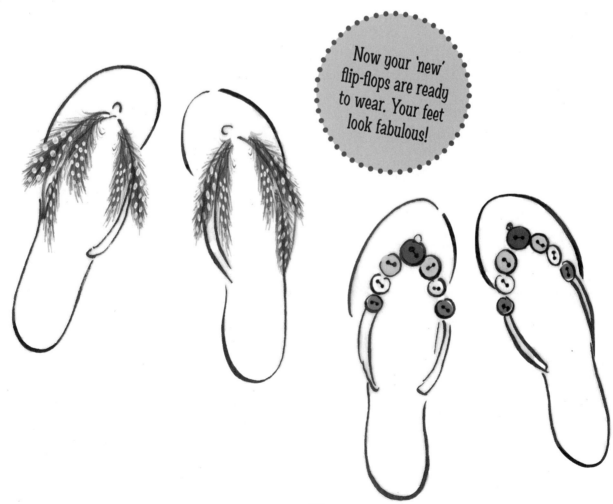

10 things to do... for a make-over

Do you feel like trying a brand-new look? Or perhaps you just need pampering? Here are a few tips!

1. Photo fun!

Before you do anything, take a photo of yourself. Then you can take one after your make-over and see the difference. It's all part of the fun!

2. Singing in the shower

There's nothing more refreshing than a quick shower! So if you want to feel instantly amazing, jump under the water and pamper yourself with your favourite shower gel. And you can always practise your singing at the same time!

3. Get a hair cut!

It's the classic way to get a new look. Flick through some hairstyle magazines and pick something you like. And ask your hairdresser's opinion!

4. Hair up or down?

If you don't want to get a hair cut, you can still try out a new style. If you normally wear your hair up, try letting it down and perhaps add cute clips. Or if you wear it down, try plaits or a funky pony tail.

5. Healthy glow!

Fill a sink with warm water (make sure it's not hot). Then soak a face cloth in the water and press it to your face. Repeat two or three times. Your skin will feel refreshed and look gorgeously healthy!

6. Heavenly hands...

Soak your hands in warm water for 10 minutes. Pat them dry with a towel and then trim your nails neatly with nail clippers or scissors. Add light moisturiser or hand cream for a lovely, silky feel!

7. ... and fab feet

If you're showing off in fab flip-flops, make sure your feet are funky too! Treat your feet just like your hands. Soak them in a bowl of warm water, pat dry and then trim your nails. Add your favourite body lotion for a soft touch!

8. Pretty nails

If you're going to a party and want an extra bit of polish, don't forget your nails. Paint fingers and toes with pretty glitter varnishes or pale pink.

9. Go bargain hunting

You might need a new outfit after all that pampering! You don't always have to spend a lot to get new clothes. Look in charity shops or second-hand clothes stalls in markets. You might be surprised at what you find!

10. Keep fit and well

Finally, feeling good is all part of looking good! It's no use getting a new hair cut if you don't eat well or keep fit. Make sure you eat plenty of fruit and veg, drink water and do some exercise to help you feel fab.

At the beach

The girls spend the day at the beach to practise their dance moves! Unscramble Anna's secret message to find out their best skill!

Hint:
The words are broken up in the wrong places!

OURBE STSKI LLISKNO WIN GHOWT
OWOR KAS ATE AM

....

....

Jess and the Go Girls

The girls have got their image all worked out, thanks to Roxy. Now all they have to do is play some music. Easy, right?

PART 3

It was a gorgeous day, and the Go Girls were down at the beach. It was the kind of day that Anna normally loved best – sun, sand, surf and her best friends all together. Except today, something seemed to be wrong.

"No!" Jess exclaimed. "I really think we need lots of fast songs."

"But everyone at school thinks we should have slow ones too," said Milly.

"We ought to play stuff that's a bit softer and not so rocky," Carla said.

"It's got to be something we can dance to..." Taylor piped up.

Anna sighed to herself, *maybe this is why every band needs a manager...* She decided to take charge. "OK, girls. I think we're having what is known as 'musical differences'. Instead of focusing on what we DON'T agree on, let's find something we ALL enjoy playing. Let's look for inspiration! I'm going surfing. When I get back, hit me with a plan!"

Anna picked up her board. She paddled out to sea and breathed in the air. *I just love surfing*, she thought as she bobbed up and down, waiting for a wave to bring her back to shore.

On the beach, Milly picked up Anna's camera. She followed her friend to the edge of the sea and waited until Anna jumped up on her board. Anna bent her knees and rode the wave – she looked so powerful and elegant. Milly flicked the video button and caught Anna turning, using the energy of the wave with ease.

Milly wandered back to the others. "Thinking of inspiration, I just took a great video of Anna," she said.

The others took a look.

"Wow, she's awesome," Jess said, excitedly. "This video would make an amazing backdrop for our first gig."

"We could write some music that rolls along, like waves," Carla offered.

Just then, Anna returned, dripping with seawater. "Hey," she grinned, overhearing her friends. "I think we're getting somewhere!"

They've got the music, now what? Continued on page 74

50

Towel time

Doodle your cool designs on this big beach towel. Go for it!

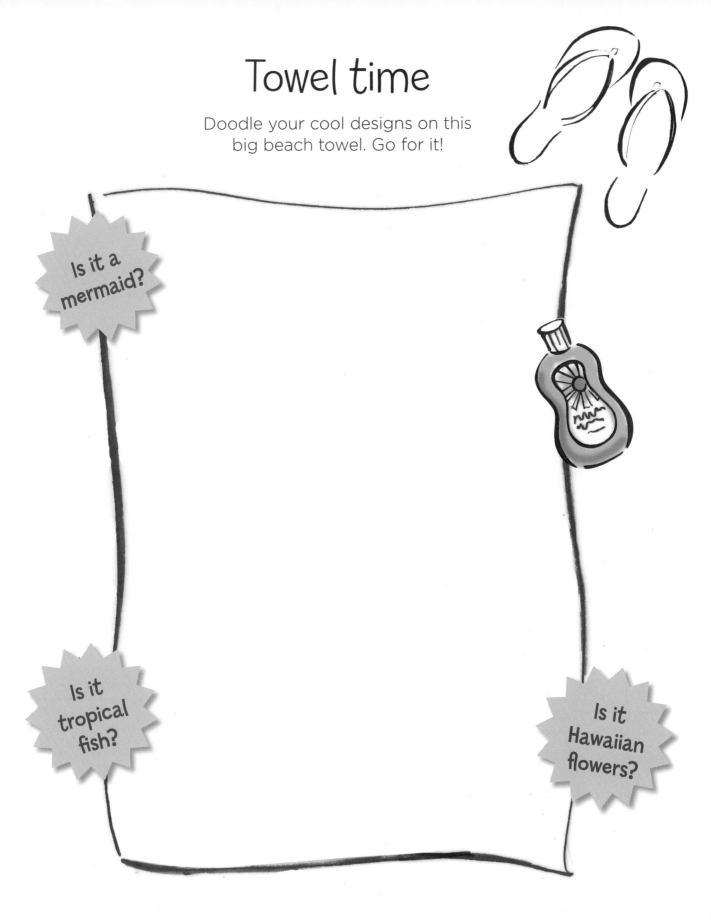

Is it a mermaid?

Is it tropical fish?

Is it Hawaiian flowers?

Spot the difference

There are ten tricky differences between the two pictures of the girls at the beach. Ring them when you've got them!

Are you busy on the beach?

So how do you entertain yourself all day on the beach?
Do this quiz and find out what you're best at.

Do you love relaxing?
- yes
- not always

Do you spend ages deciding what to pack?
- I do!
- not really

Do you like messing around in the waves?
- yuck!
- splash!

Do you stop off at the newsstand for a magazine?
- totally
- sometimes

Is your swimsuit the latest style?
- of course
- last year's

Is lying in the sun a bit boring?
- yes
- no

Is going for a swim too much effort?
- yep
- nope

Are you any good at daydreaming?
- the best!
- too busy

If you see a ball, do you want to kick it?
- not always
- definitely

Is jewellery an essential item?
- no
- yes

Are you always reading, even when your friends are in the water?
- no
- absolutely

Is going for a run lots of fun?
- not really
- loads

BEACH BEAUTY

You love beach glamour! With a matching beach bag and towel, and super cool sunglasses, you've got style!

BEACH BOOKWORM

For you, a day at the beach is one big opportunity to catch up on your reading. Turn that page, girl!

BEACH BALL PLAYER

You love a sporty challenge. Whether it's beach cricket or beach volleyball, you're ready to play the game.

Mates in a maze

Anna has to collect all her friends together so they can practise their show. Go round the maze and collect them all!

Puzzle parade

Anna needs to get to Windy Beach, which line leads her there?

A
B
C

NORTH BEACH

WINDY BEACH

BAY BEACH

Only two of these music players are an exact match. Which ones?

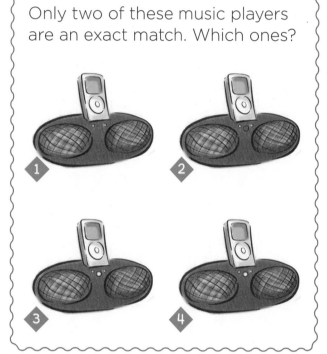

1
2
3
4

Unscramble the letters to reveal Anna's favourite hobby.

F R U N

I S G

Write the answer here

Beach babes

Find the beachy words in the grid. Look up, down, backwards, across and diagonally.

S	K	C	O	R	S	E	T	P	O	S	E
W	A	H	I	C	K	I	A	N	U	R	S
Y	D	N	O	N	U	D	U	I	E	P	W
O	D	G	D	S	D	E	Y	L	O	E	I
N	L	I	M	L	K	U	T	E	F	B	M
B	W	I	I	I	B	S	E	W	I	B	M
S	W	N	A	N	A	S	A	O	S	L	I
S	G	L	I	C	R	G	L	T	H	E	N
C	S	I	D	O	C	E	N	L	H	S	G
A	D	N	R	W	A	V	E	S	E	H	N
D	A	T	G	N	I	F	R	U	S	H	G
S	S	E	V	O	O	H	E	M	A	L	S

Draw Anna!

Copy Anna's picture into the grid, square by square.

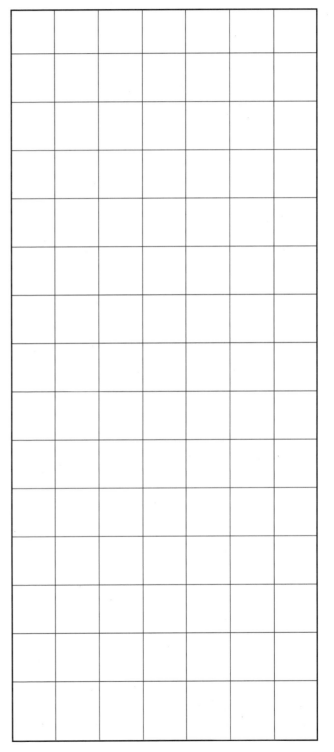

Lost it!

Anna has lost her belongings on the beach and everything looks the same! Look at the clues opposite and help her find them.

Clues

1. Anna's towel has two palm trees.
2. She left her flowery flip-flops on the towel.
3. She didn't leave her sun cream on the towel, but she did leave her sunglasses.
4. She left her beach ball behind, too.

58

In the swim

The girls are going for a swim. But who's wearing what? Work it out by reading the clues and putting a tick for yes, or a cross for no, in each box.

Clues

1. Roxy's swimsuit is orange but it doesn't have animals on it.
2. The pink swimsuit, which does not have flowers on it, is worn by Jess.
3. The swimsuit with fish on it is not worn by Anna.
4. The flowery swimsuit is not blue.

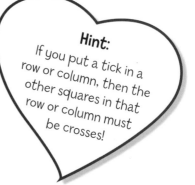

Hint:
If you put a tick in a row or column, then the other squares in that row or column must be crosses!

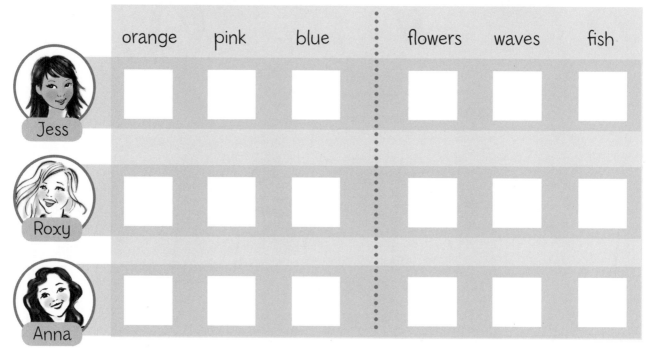

	Colour			Pattern		
	orange	pink	blue	flowers	waves	fish
Jess						
Roxy						
Anna						

60

Puzzle parade

Count the fish in this pattern.
Look carefully!

It's 9.15am and Anna is leaving home. It takes:

20 minutes to get to the beach

15 minutes to buy juices at the café

5 minutes to walk to her favourite spot

2 minutes to unpack her bag

8 minutes to get the music ready

Now answer the questions:

What time does Anna finish?

....

She's meeting the other girls on the beach at 10am. Is she ready on time?

....

Anna's challenge

Next time you're at the beach, challenge your friends to some fun games!

Sandcastle surprise

Split into small teams, or you can do this individually if you like. Then choose a theme, such as animals, sea creatures or famous buildings. Each team has 20 minutes to make the best sand sculpture relating to the theme!

Digging race

Challenge your friends to dig a hole and fill it with water. The one to fill their hole first wins. Sounds easy? Actually, it can be pretty hard but you'll have a lot of fun trying!

Make a sandman

Ever made a snowman? Split into teams and make sandmen instead! Make sure the sand is very wet so that you can build your sandman up really high. The winners are the ones who build the biggest. Use pebbles and sticks for faces and arms.

Beach comber hunt

Make a list of ten things that are commonly found on the beach, such as seaweed, pebbles, shells, sand, driftwood etc. Give your friends 20 minutes to go and find everything on the list. The winner is the one who gets back first.

!
Don't forget!
It's easy to get lost on a beach. Remember not to wander off alone – stay in sight of your friends!

Seaweed
Driftwood
Pebbles

Cute costume!

Doodle a fun pattern on
Anna's new swimsuit!

Is it
splashy?

Is it
surfy?

Is it sporty
or cute?

Cool surfboards

Surfboards come in all sorts of patterns.
Design two cool ones here!

What's the job?

Unscramble these letters to find the names of four jobs Anna might want to do when she grows up. Then find them in the grid!

FIGLARDUE

....

FURSRE

....

CORKRAST

....

NAMAREG

....

C	S	H	O	R	S	E	B	L
K	U	H	I	C	K	M	I	N
Y	R	N	O	N	K	F	U	I
O	F	G	T	T	E	E	Y	D
N	E	R	E	G	A	N	A	M
B	R	L	U	I	R	B	E	R
C	L	A	A	N	I	M	A	E
U	R	A	T	S	K	C	O	R
D	S	I	O	O	K	E	N	F
A	D	A	R	S	O	F	A	H

Catch a wave!

Anna is surfing in a competition! Help her catch the best wave and get back to the beach, scoring as many points as possible. But no going back on yourself!

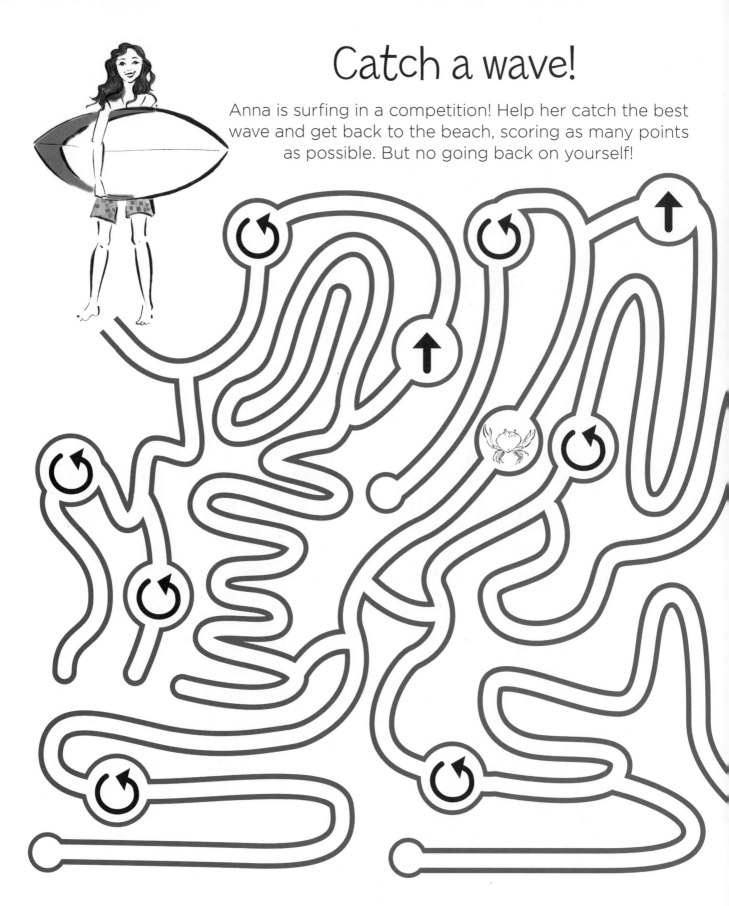

How to score points

Ride over a crab
Take away 1 point

Catch the big wave
5 points

Do a turn
1 point

Do a jump
3 points

big wave

67

Anna's ideas!

While they were at the beach, the girls had lots of ideas for the music for their band's songs. Help Anna write down the sounds, sights and sensations that might inspire them!

Beachy music
Waves crashing
People having fun
Seagulls flying

Festival music

Relaxing music

Party music

Design Anna's outfit

Design an outfit for Anna. What's her style?

Sarong over a swimsuit?

Fill it in!

What logo would Anna like best on a t-shirt?

Board shorts and a surf t-shirt?

Puzzle parade

Look at these six pictures of Anna's sun cream.
Which is the odd one out?

1  2 3

4 5 6

Anna loves surfing! Put these surfing activities in order from first to last.

Jog to the sea ( )

Paddle away from the beach ( )

Ride the waves! ( )

Wax the board ( )

70

Sunny shirt!

Use this easy tie-dye method to make a sunburst pattern shirt. All tie-dye patterns are unique – so no one else will have one quite like yours!

You will need

* A tie-dye kit from a craft shop
* A white cotton t-shirt or vest
* Rubber bands
* A marble
* Rubber gloves
* Tap water

1 Ask an adult to help you follow the instructions on the tie-dye kit. Always wear rubber gloves when handling dye.

2 Bunch up the centre of your top around a marble. Now add rubber bands to form a tube, as shown.

3 Now place in the dye for at least 20 minutes. The longer you leave it, the darker the colour will be.

4 Take out of the dye and rinse in cold water. Wring it out, then remove the rubber bands and marble. Your sunburst design will appear!

Wash according to the instructions on the kit... and soon your sunny t-shirt will be ready to wear!

71

10 things to... create a band

Anna has been voted the band manager. Here are ten things that YOU could do if you want to start your own band!

1. Pick your personnel

Every band needs different members - musical, creative and people who are good at organising! Get together with your band and decide who does what. If there's someone missing, such as a great singer, find one!

2. What are your influences?

Everyone likes different kinds of music, but you need to agree what kind of music you want to play. Listen to everyone's favourite tracks and discuss what you'd like YOUR band to sound like.

3. Get some inspiration

Ideas are all around you! Listen to music, look at art, talk to friends, go outside for a walk – anything that makes you feel something can be an inspiration for a good song.

4. Who writes the songs?

Making up your own music and lyrics is all part of being in a band. But covering other band's songs can also be a good way to start playing together.

5. Get styled up!

A cool band needs a cool image! Which one of your members has great fashion sense or has a cool individual style? Make her the band's stylist!

6. Practise playing!

Get together regularly and learn how to play and sing together. You can practise your dance moves, too! When you feel confident, play to a small group of friends and listen to their comments - you might learn from them.

7. Shoot a video

Get together and have some fun by shooting videos for your songs. Perform your dance moves, play your song or just mess around together!

8. Create a fan page

To keep your friends updated, create a fan page on the web. You can post your songs and videos, plus any news that you want people to hear about - such as when you're playing your next gig!

9. Enter a competition

If there are any local talent shows happening, enter your band. There's nothing like the experience of playing that first gig!

10. Send out a demo

And when you're really confident, you could send out a demo tape to a record company or go for an audition... you never know where it might lead to! Good luck!

Picnic party

Milly organises a picnic for the Go Girls, so they can practise their act!
Can you work out what Milly's secret message says?

13.25
6.1.22.5
16.9.3.14.9.3
6.15.15.4
9.19
3.21.16.3.1.11.5.19

Hint:
A=1 and Z=26

Jess and the Go Girls

The band is taking shape. Milly decides to host a picnic in the park, just to iron out a few details – like the dance routine!

Milly spread out the picnic blanket under the shade of a tree on the edge of the park. She laid out the food she'd brought along – sandwiches, popcorn and freshly-baked cookies, complete with home-made smoothies. She knew exactly the kind of food her friends loved best.

Soon the rest of the girls arrived and they all sat down for a feast before the hard work began. They talked as they ate and Anna scribbled notes in her pad.

"OK," she began when the last cookie had gone. "Let's recap. We play a couple of Star Rock's songs, then we move onto our own song *Catch a Wave*. Great lyrics, Milly, by the way! All we need now is a routine for the backing singers – that's me and Roxy – to perform during the

guitar part. Taylor, can you take us through a few ideas?"

Taylor got up and flicked on the music. The sound of Star Rock filled the air and Taylor began to dance. The backing singers joined in and soon a routine was starting to flow.

"Carla, do you want to add your lead vocals?" Anna called. But Carla wasn't listening.

"Look," she said, pointing behind the tree. "I think that little dog wants to have a nibble at our picnic!"

The girls looked over to see a thin, black puppy, edging towards the blanket. "Oh, he looks so hungry," Carla sighed. "He has no collar – it looks like he's been abandoned."

Anna smiled. She knew Carla had a whole bunch of pets at home – and kept badgering her parents for more!

"I'm going to take him to the pet rescue centre. Sorry to stop the band practice, girls," Carla said as she whisked up the puppy in her arms.

Jess frowned as Carla disappeared. "But she's the lead. We need her."

Anna nodded. "Let's save it for another day. I guess she has to do the right thing..."

Carla has a surprise for the girls...
Continued on page 98

Ice cream dream

Lucky you, there's an ice-cream stall in the park! Draw a yummy ice cream with oodles of toppings in this double cone!

Sauce AND sprinkles?

Different flavours?

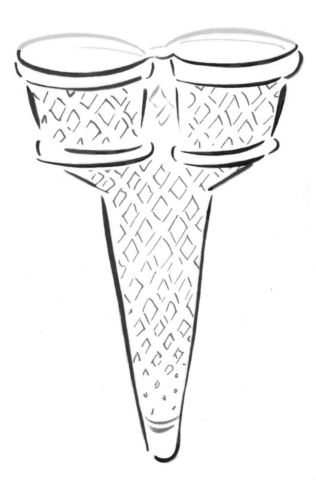

Crumbled brownie bits?

75

Spot the difference

There are ten tricky differences between these pictures of the girls in the park. Ring them when you've got them.

True or false?

Milly loves cooking! She's got 12 top facts about food – but only some of them are true. Can you spot the false ones?

1. Cupcakes get their name because they were made in cups.

☐ TRUE ☐ FALSE

5. Baked beans are good for you.

☐ TRUE ☐ FALSE

9. Vanilla is the most popular ice-cream flavour in the world.

☐ TRUE ☐ FALSE

2. A top Japanese food is 'sashimi', or raw sliced meat.

☐ TRUE ☐ FALSE

6. Yoghurt is made from honey and water.

☐ TRUE ☐ FALSE

10. Raisins are really dried grapes.

☐ TRUE ☐ FALSE

3. It takes between 3 and 6 minutes to boil an egg.

☐ TRUE ☐ FALSE

7. There are around 7,500 different types of apple.

☐ TRUE ☐ FALSE

11. A 'knickerbocker glory' is a type of very smelly cheese.

☐ TRUE ☐ FALSE

4. The French word baguette means 'funny bread'.

☐ TRUE ☐ FALSE

8. Olives are tiny fish that live in the sea.

☐ TRUE ☐ FALSE

12. Some types of carrot are purple.

☐ TRUE ☐ FALSE

Cupcake caper

Go across the picnic blanket, collecting all the cakes. You can only step on each square once and you can't move diagonally. Don't tread on the cups!

Milly's challenge

A picnic is more fun when there are games to play too!
Try these three guessing games at your picnic party.

Who am I?
One girl thinks of a person
– maybe a famous person, or someone
you all know. The other players take
turns to ask questions that will help them
guess who it is. But the first girl can
only answer 'yes' or 'no'.

Guess the word
One girl covers her ears while the
others agree on a feeling (for instance, happy).
She must ask each player in turn to
do something, such as eat a crisp, in 'the manner
of the word' (for instance, happily). The first girl
then tries to guess the describing word.
Have a go - pretend to eat a crisp happily!

Squeak, piggy, squeak!
One girl shuts her eyes. The other
players stand in a circle around her.
The first girl must catch hold of another
player and say 'Squeak, piggy, squeak!'
The player squeaks, and the first girl
must guess who it is.

Picnic puzzle

Find the picnic words in the grid. Look up, down, backwards, across and diagonally.

Word list

basket	games
blanket	park
cakes	picnic
drinks	plates
friends	sandwiches
fruit	sunny

C	S	P	O	S	D	P	R	H	I	R	B
K	C	L	I	C	R	M	D	G	U	A	Z
Y	D	A	O	N	I	R	U	G	S	S	A
O	E	T	K	R	N	L	D	K	E	H	G
N	F	E	T	E	K	L	E	H	Y	B	A
P	R	S	E	I	S	T	C	N	N	H	U
C	I	D	A	N	I	I	Y	E	N	A	M
U	E	C	E	T	W	A	T	I	U	R	F
J	N	E	N	D	O	N	Q	H	S	T	K
A	D	A	N	I	G	A	M	E	S	H	R
D	S	A	A	L	C	L	Q	S	N	L	A
H	S	E	T	E	K	N	A	L	B	Q	P

Draw Milly!

Copy Milly's picture into the grid, square by square.

Sunshine and showers

This is a game for two players. Start at number 1. Take it in turns to roll a die and move around the board, using coins or small charms as counters. Follow the key opposite!

83

Super duper sudoku

This sudoku is super dooper tricky. You have to get all the numbers from 1 to 9 in the right place in every 3 x 3 square, row and column. Good luck!

3			8		7		9	
5	1	7	2					
4		8			6			5
7	4		5				1	2
	2		7	6	9		4	
8	3				1		5	6
			6			5		7
6					2	8	3	
	7		9		5			1

Getting stuck?

Here are some clues to get you started:

✳ The middle box in the bottom row is missing a number 7. There's only one place it could go...

✳ The box on the bottom left is quite empty. But it should be easy to place number 8 in there, if you check out the rows and columns around it.

✳ The middle box on the right needs a number 7. Look at the where the 7s are in the other middle boxes and you'll see where it should go.

Puzzle parade

Which shadow matches Milly exactly?

1

2

3

4

Milly has written a list of cool song titles, but they are back to front. Can you work out what they are without using a mirror?

BEST FRIENDS FOREVER!

....

....

GET READY TO GO GIRLS!

....

....

DANCE TO THE
CRAZY BEAT!

....

....

Picnic plate

Mmmm! What would you have on your plate to make a perfect picnic? Draw it in here!

Is it a wrap or a roll?

What's your fab filling?

What's your fave fruit?

Milly's lyrics

Milly loves writing poems and stories – so the girls ask her if she can write some cool lyrics for their song. Why don't you give it a try, too?

Title:

Come up with a catchy title for your song!

Verse:

How does the song get started?

Chorus:

The chorus is what people often remember - so make it a good one!

Now you're in the swing of it, write a few more verses!

Ice cream inventions!

Make up a name for a new ice-cream flavour!
Pick one word from each column and write it in below.
Get your best friend to do the same, then have another go!

Triple	Fudge	Delight
Totally	Chocolate	Moments
Mega	Mint	Sensation
Very	Berry	Explosion
Cool	Vanilla	Dream

You

....

....

You

....

....

Your best friend

....

....

Your best friend

....

....

Design Milly's outfit

Design an outfit for Milly. She's the creative one, so make her look arty!

What about a big hat or sunglasses?

How about a fun, fruity pattern?

Fill it in!

What would Milly wear in her hair?

....

....

....

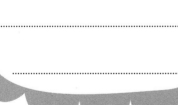

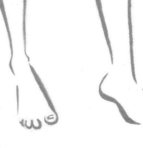

Puzzle parade

Milly loves food and she's set her friends a fruity challenge. Only three of these are the names of real fruit. Which are the fakes?

Horned Melon
☐ TRUE ☐ FALSE

Starfruit
☐ TRUE ☐ FALSE

Song Berry
☐ TRUE ☐ FALSE

Guitarna
☐ TRUE ☐ FALSE

Tear Pear
☐ TRUE ☐ FALSE

Dragon Fruit
☐ TRUE ☐ FALSE

Milly is buying her friends a sweet treat. Rearrange the letters in the grid to find out what. Write it below.

C	A	L
O	C	H
T	E	O

How many other words can you make from these letters?

....

....

....

....

....

....

....

Work it out!

At the picnic, the girls each picked a different favourite food and sang a different number of songs. Use the clues to put ticks and crosses in the columns and find out what they were!

Clues

1. Roxy sang four songs and ate grapes.
2. Anna sang twice as many songs as Carla.
3. Carla's favourite food was not the smoothies.
4. The girl who sang the most songs liked the smoothies.
5. Jess's favourite food was the sandwiches. She sang half as many songs as Roxy.
6. The cupcakes were Taylor's favourite food.

Hint
If you put a tick in a row, then the other squares in that row must be crosses!

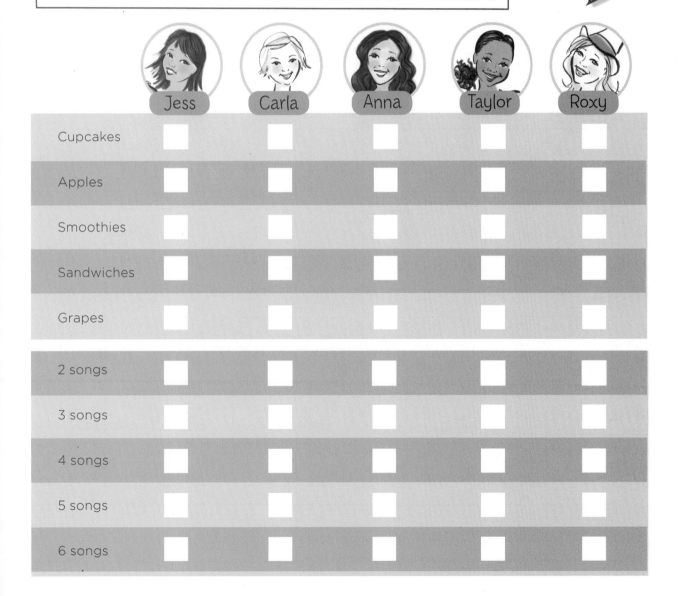

	Jess	Carla	Anna	Taylor	Roxy
Cupcakes	☐	☐	☐	☐	☐
Apples	☐	☐	☐	☐	☐
Smoothies	☐	☐	☐	☐	☐
Sandwiches	☐	☐	☐	☐	☐
Grapes	☐	☐	☐	☐	☐
2 songs	☐	☐	☐	☐	☐
3 songs	☐	☐	☐	☐	☐
4 songs	☐	☐	☐	☐	☐
5 songs	☐	☐	☐	☐	☐
6 songs	☐	☐	☐	☐	☐

Lost!

The picnic has been packed up, but Milly has lost something. Move around the park, following the directions and find out what it is! Use the compass to help you.

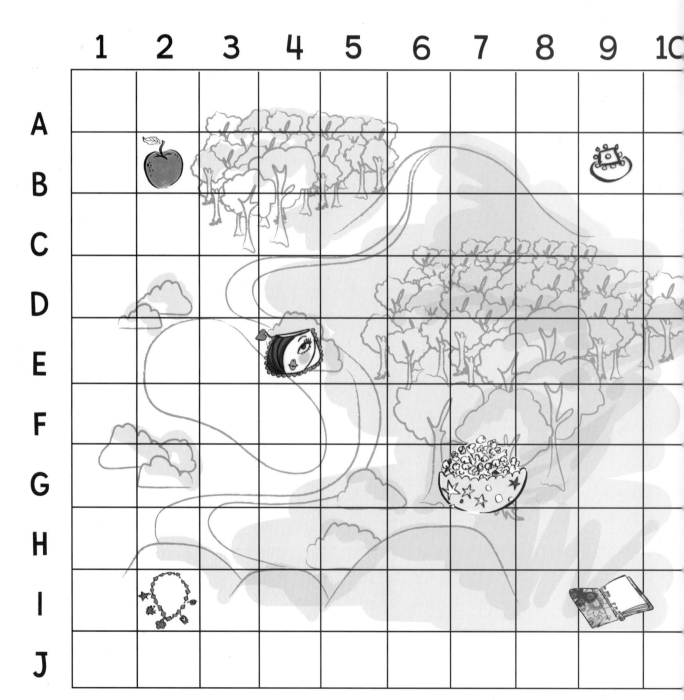

Directions

Start at 3 squares to the south of the apple
Go 4 squares east
Go 2 squares south
Go 1 square west
Go 5 squares north

Go 10 squares east
Go 1 square north
Go 3 squares west
Go 3 squares south
Go 4 squares east
Go 2 squares south

Write Milly's lost item here:

....

| 11 | 12 | 13 | 14 | 15 | 16 | 17 | 18 | 19 | 20 |

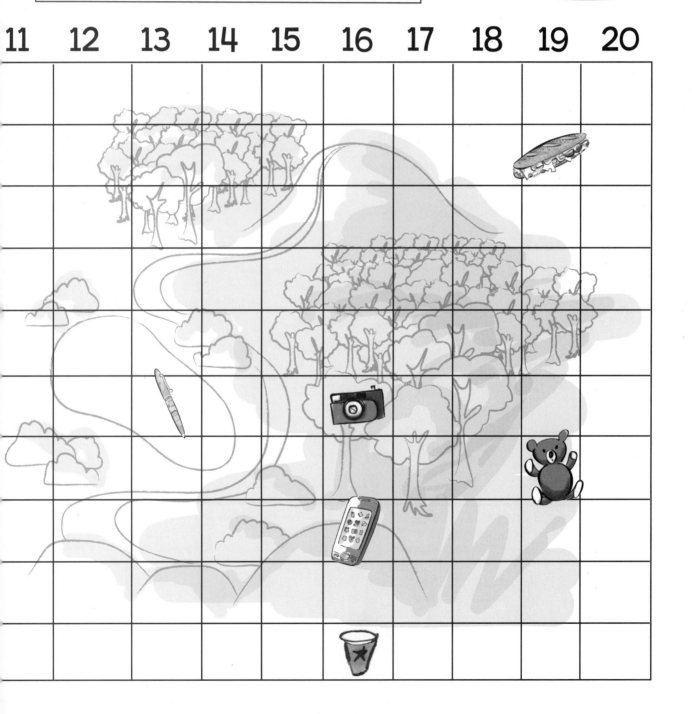

93

Puzzle parade

Six of these baguettes are exactly the same. Circle the two that are different from the rest.

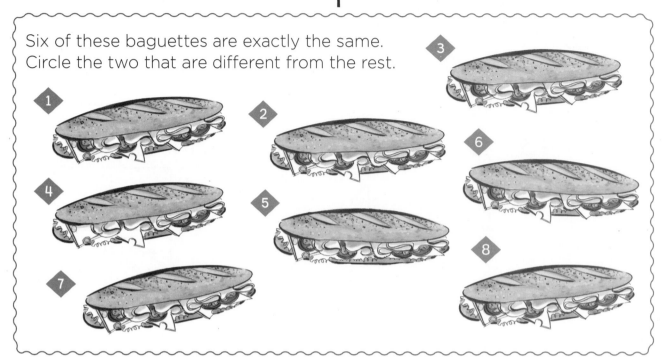

Jess, Milly and Anna are playing cards. Who has the hand with the most points? Look at the key to help you.

Key

Star = 1 point
Rainbow = 2 points
Musical note = 3 points

Cupcake creations

Turn plain cupcakes into the main attraction by decorating them in fun ways! You can use ready-made cakes for this activity.

You will need

* Ready-made plain cupcakes
* Tubes of different coloured icing
* Assorted cake decorations, such as jelly sweets, sprinkles or chocolate chips

1 Funny faces
Ice the cupcakes. For each cake, add decorations, such as jelly sweets, to make eyes and a nose. Use sprinkles for hair and a row of silver balls for a mouth. Make them all different!

2 Fab flower
Put a cupcake in the middle of a plate. Now place six cupcakes around it to look like petals. Ice the 'petals' in pale pink and add sprinkles. Then ice the middle cake in a darker colour.

3 Mega messages
Use your cupcakes to spell out a fun message, such as 'friends forever'. Ice each cake in a pale colour, then use tubes of dark icing to add a letter on top of each one.

If you're feeling creative, make a small bee out of marzipan and put it on one of the petals!

95

10 things to do...
for a picnic party!

Are you having a picnic party? Here are some ideas to make it go with a swing!

1. Location, location

First decide where you are going to have your picnic. Will it be in a local park or a picnic party in your back garden? Make sure that you have a back-up plan in case of rain!

2. Set the scene

You'll need to bring one or two large picnic rugs, depending on the number of guests. Pick a spot near a shady tree and hang some bunting in the branches. Add a few cushions around the picnic blanket for extra comfort!

3. Cups and plates

Pack pretty paper cups and plates instead of heavy dishes you will have to carry home. This will also mean that you don't have to do any washing up and nothing will get broken! If you want to be green, pick recycled paper.

4. Finger foods

There's no need to carry cutlery when you make up a picnic of finger foods. Here are some ideas: cherry tomatoes, cocktail sausages, boiled eggs, carrot sticks with dips, sausage rolls, small slices of cold pizza, cubes of cheese and crisps.

5. Something different

Make your sandwiches memorable to munch! Use cookie cutters to cut them into pretty shapes, such as hearts and stars. Or make rolled sandwiches by spreading a piece of bread with cream cheese, then rolling it and cutting it into slices.

6. Pack it all in

Carry a cooler that is the right size for the number of people that you are inviting. If it is a picnic for two you don't need anything too big and bulky. If it is a large group do not try to stuff all the picnic items into one small cooler.

7. Choose a tune

Bring a small music player that runs on batteries and pick some funky background music to play. If you are in the park, keep the volume low – not everyone will want to hear your tunes!

8. Little extras

Make sure you pack a bottle of sun cream for everyone to use. Nobody wants to get sunburn on a picnic! Another good thing to have on hand is a pack of wet wipes and paper towels for those sticky fingers.

9. Party puddings

Cupcakes with pretty icing are always a winner. But have you thought of making fruit kebabs with little marshmallows? Or how about a tub of strawberries with chocolate sauce to dip them in?

10. Fun and games

Why not bring a few things to play with after the food is finished. A Frisbee, a bat and ball, or a hula hoop are all good fun. Or you can just get your dancing shoes on like Milly and her friends!

Pet rescue

Carla loves helping out at her local pet rescue centre.
Can you unscramble her secret message?

LP YA NI WG TI PH PU IP SE
SI UJ TS HT BE SE FT NU!

Hint:
Switch round each pair of letters, then find the words!

....

....

Jess and the Go Girls

Carla has a surprise waiting for her
friends... but now she's too busy to
concentrate on the band. How can the
girls get their lead singer back?

PART 5

The girls were at the pet rescue centre, chatting as they went along the rows of pens, looking at the cute rabbits and the purring cats. Carla was brimming with pride as she continued with her story, "... and then the manager at the centre said that they would keep him until he's better. After that, mum says I can bring him home and he's going to be all mine! Until then, I can come here every day and take him for a walk."

"What are you going to call him?" Anna asked. She was pleased for her friend. Carla was obviously nuts about the little puppy.

"Lucky!" replied Carla. "Don't you think it suits him?"

But Jess was sighing under her breath – she was worried. "Carla?" she interrupted. "Do you think you have time for band practice next week?"

"Oh, I don't think so," Carla replied. "Lucky will be coming home and he's going to need lots of attention. I'm so excited!"

They stopped at Lucky's

pen and he jumped up at Carla straight away. "See, he loves me already!" Carla exclaimed. She put him on the lead and the girls started walking to the exercise field.

Anna gave Jess a quick hug. "Don't worry, Jess," she whispered. "We'll get the band back together somehow."

It was soon time to leave and the girls began the short walk home through the park. Before long, they saw Eve and Sadie jogging towards them. "Hey, we came to look for you," Eve called. "There's another music festival on next month – and there's a contest for young bands. We think you should enter! But you'll have to practise really hard to be ready."

Jess smiled at Carla. "What about it, Carla?" she asked. "You're the lead singer. We really need you to be involved."

Carla hesitated. She didn't want to let her friends down. But Lucky needed her too... What should she do?

Will the band enter the contest? Read the final part on page 122!

98

Poodle oodle doodle

If you were to discover a weird
new animal, what would it be?

Is it
fierce?

What would
you call it?

Is it cute
and fluffy?

Spot the difference

There are ten tricky differences between the pictures
of Carla and Milly walking the dogs. Ring them when you've got them.

A

B

What's your best pet?

Read these questions and circle your answers.
Then find out what kind of pet would suit you best!

1 **Your favourite pastime is:**
A. Going for long walks
B. Sitting down in a cosy chair
C. Playing in the garden

2 **The pet name that appeals to you most is:**
A. Rufus
B. Felix
C. Dandelion

3 **The thing you want most from a pet is:**
A. Friendship
B. Fun
C. Cuddles

4 **Your favourite outdoor game is:**
A. Playing catch
B. Playing 'it'
C. Playing hopscotch

5 **The sweetest thing in the world is:**
A. Big eyes and a wet nose
B. Soft fur and a cute nose
C. Long ears and a twitchy nose

6 **You could put up with a pet that:**
A. Dribbles over you!
B. Scratches the furniture!
C. Gnaws everything!

Read your results!

Mostly As
DOG DAYS
Dogs need plenty of attention but they give you lots of love in return. This one's for you!

Mostly Bs
COOL CATS
Sometimes, cats only want you when it suits them. They can be fun but also a bit cool. You'll like that!

Mostly Cs
RABBIT FANATIC
Rabbits are cute and cuddly and are fun to watch. That will suit you just fine!

Puppy trouble

Carla's new puppy is giving her the run-around!
Help her find him and pick up all the bones he's
left behind on the way.

start

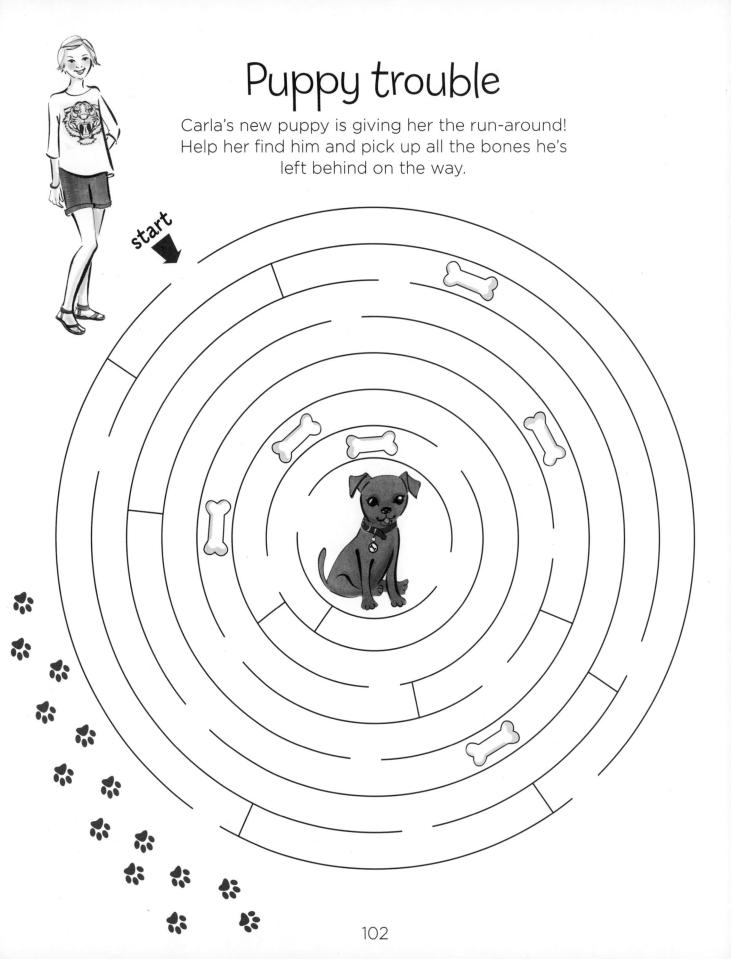

Puzzle parade

How many girl's names can you think of beginning with C? Write them down!

Carla

Carla needs to call the pet rescue centre at exactly 10am.

It's 9.30am but her phone is lost. She spends 8 minutes looking for it.

She finds it! Then Anna calls and chats for 18 minutes.

Carla spends 3 minutes looking for the right number.

Does Carla manage to make the call on time? Tick the box.

☐ yes ☐ no

What's that noise?

Woof!

Purr!

Tweet!

Tweet!

Find the pet noises in the grid.
Look up, down, backwards,
across and diagonally.

Word List

bark	neigh	squawk
bray	purr	tweet
chirp	sniff	woof
meow	squeak	yap

C	R	R	U	P	S	E	B	S	O	S	E
K	A	H	I	C	K	M	D	Q	U	R	H
Y	F	F	I	N	S	E	U	U	H	P	F
A	D	G	T	T	K	O	Y	E	O	H	P
R	L	A	S	E	K	W	Y	A	G	A	J
B	E	S	D	Q	O	B	T	K	Y	H	B
S	Q	N	A	O	U	M	A	E	N	A	M
U	L	E	F	P	T	A	A	L	E	O	P
S	S	I	O	R	K	E	W	F	H	W	R
A	D	G	R	I	B	A	R	K	N	H	T
D	Z	H	Q	H	I	A	N	Y	N	L	G
H	S	E	V	C	O	Y	E	M	A	L	S

Draw Carla!

Copy Carla's picture into the grid, square by square.

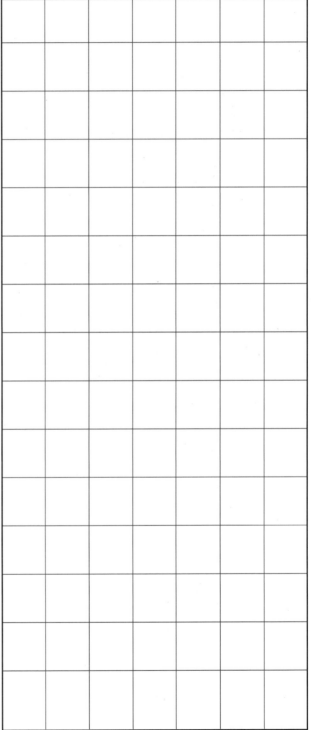

Animal alphabet

Look at the clues and then fill in the answers to this animal alphabet quiz.

Clues

A It eats ants

B It hangs upside down

C A very popular pet

D It's a bit like a horse and it brays

E The largest animal on land

F An insect that glows

G An African animal with a long neck

H A cute pet that nibbles

I A lizard with spines running down its back

J A kind of wild dog

K A large bird from New Zealand that can't fly

L A pretty, spotty insect

M A large, noisy parrot

N An undersea creature with a long horn on its nose

O A giant ape that lives in the rainforest

P A bird with a fan of beautiful tail feathers

Q A little bird, often kept on a farm

R A big African animal with a horn on its nose

S A fierce fish with sharp teeth

T A big, hairy spider

U This animal only exists in fairytales and stories

V A snake with a dangerous bite

W It's like a kangaroo but smaller

X A Mexican dog with no hair

Y A big, hairy cow-like animal that lives in Asia

Z It's a fish with black-and-white stripes

Tip:
Some of these answers are a bit tricky. You're allowed three internet searches to help you!

Answers

A ....

B ....

C ....

D ....

E ....

F ....

G ....

H ....

I ....

J ....

K ....

L ....

M ....

N ....

O ....

P ....

Q ....

R ....

S ....

T ....

U ....

V ....

W ....

X ....

y ....

z ....

Fill it in!

Which of these animals would you most like to meet?

....

Carla's challenge

Take it in turns with a friend to look at this picture of Carla's pets for 20 seconds. Then cover up the picture and answer the questions below. Who got the most right?

		Your best friend	You
1	How many pets were there altogether?		
2	How many bowls were there?		
3	Did the cat have a collar?		
4	Was there a white mouse?		
5	Did the rabbit have spots?		

Secret scribbles

Carla is writing in code in her diary, so that her little brother can't read what she thinks! Can you decode her secret thoughts?

The code

A	B	C	D	E	F	G	H	I	J	K	L	M	N	O	P	Q	R	S	T	U	V	W	X	Y	Z
✖	✚	✜	✤	✥	◆	◇	★	☆	✪	☆	★	★	☆	★	☆	✴	✳	✶	✷	✸	✺	✹	✦	✵	✺

Write the answer here:

....

....

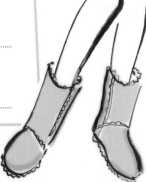

109

Puzzle parade

Which of these pictures of Carla are exactly the same?

1

2

3

4

Which of these pictures of Carla's microphone is the odd one out?

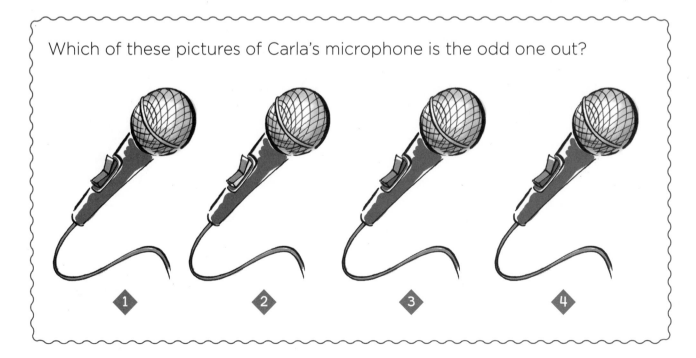

1

2

3

4

Butterfly doodle

Butterflies are symmetrical – they have the same pattern on both sides. Doodle a beautiful one here!

Is it spotty?

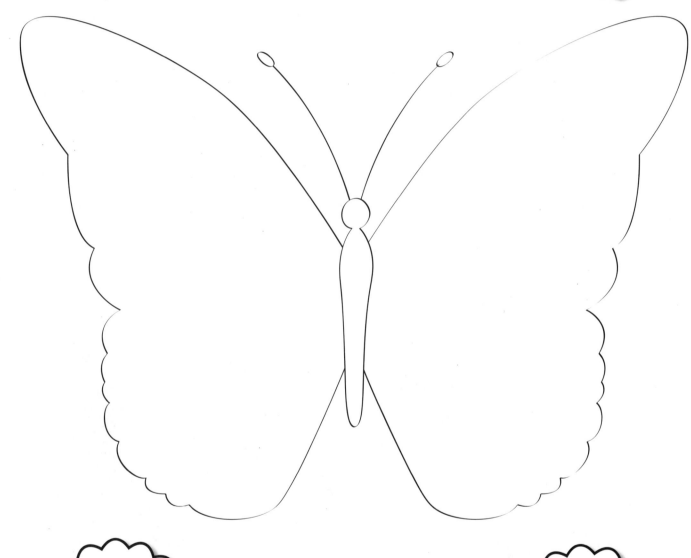

What colour is its body?

Are the wings brightly coloured?

Puzzle parade

Carla is the lead singer in the band. How many words can you make out of the letters in the word MICROPHONE?

....
....
....
....
....
....
....

1-5
See if you can find a few more!

6-10
You're pretty good at this! Well done.

11-14
Wow! Sing out your success!

Which shadow exactly matches this picture of Carla's rabbit?

Web wander

Move around this web and spell out the name of Carla's favourite creepy crawly. Start at the arrow and move one space at a time in any direction, except diagonally. You must finish at the letter in the centre of the web.

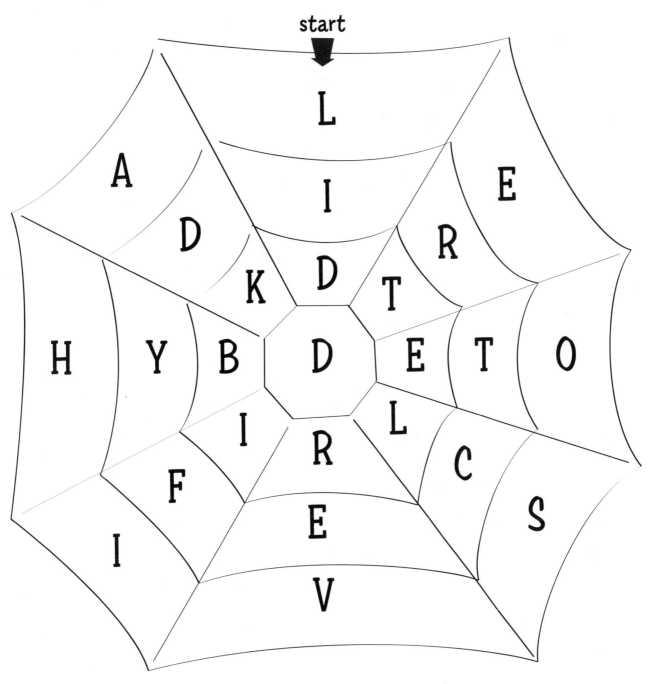

What's your singing style?

If you were a famous singer, would you be a star solo artist or would you be in a hit girl group? Answer the questions and follow the arrows to find out!

start

You're the kind of girl who always likes to hang around with a bunch of friends!

not always

yes

One of your favourite sayings is 'Let's go, girls!'

yep!

nah!

You like to copy your friends' fashion ideas!

never!

of course

not necessarily

You think it's better to go shoe shopping on your own!

You like to have a very best friend around, who always thinks like you do!

always

no way

yes!

not really

Your dream is to be school captain or team leader at your local club!

One of your favourite sayings is 'Look at me!'

nope!

yes

absolutely

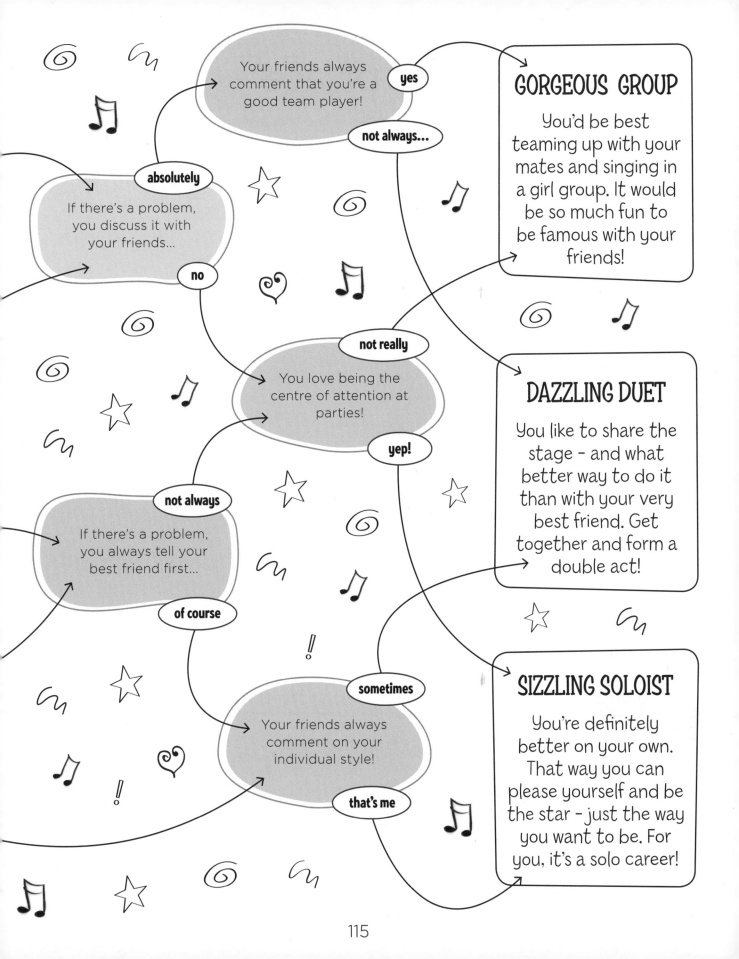

Your friends always comment that you're a good team player!

yes

not always...

absolutely

If there's a problem, you discuss it with your friends...

no

GORGEOUS GROUP

You'd be best teaming up with your mates and singing in a girl group. It would be so much fun to be famous with your friends!

not really

You love being the centre of attention at parties!

yep!

not always

If there's a problem, you always tell your best friend first...

of course

DAZZLING DUET

You like to share the stage – and what better way to do it than with your very best friend. Get together and form a double act!

sometimes

Your friends always comment on your individual style!

that's me

SIZZLING SOLOIST

You're definitely better on your own. That way you can please yourself and be the star – just the way you want to be. For you, it's a solo career!

115

Pet palace

Do you love pets? Why not design
a luxury home for your very own
animal best friend?

Fill it in!

What kind of pet is it?

What luxurious items
does it need?

What's your pet
palace called?

Design Carla's outfit

Design an outfit for Carla to wear as lead singer!

Is her top pretty or funky?

Are her shoes made for walking or dancing?

Fill it in!

What's YOUR favourite footwear?

117

Puzzle parade

Unscramble the letters to work out the names of Carla's other pets.

AQEUKS

....

INGEGR

....

RYENH

....

Which picture of Carla's puppy is the odd one out?

How many times can you find the word DOG? Look up, down, across, backwards and diagonally.

D	O	G	O	D
G	O	D	O	G
G	O	D	G	O
O	G	O	D	G
D	D	G	O	D

Make a spotty bug

Make a cute cuddly toy to decorate your room or give to your best friend! Try out this spotty bug...

You will need

* Scissors
* Felt material in assorted colours, plus old scraps
* Large sewing needle
* Embroidery thread
* 4 black pipecleaners from a craft kit
* Fabric glue

Top tips!

Running stitch   Over-stitch

 1 Take a circle of felt, about the size of a dinner plate.

 2 Thread your needle and knot the thread. Using simple running stitch, sew around the outer edges of the circle and then pull the thread tight to make a ball. Don't tie the thread off just yet.

 3 Stuff the ball with lots of old scraps of material. Using over-stitch, stitch up the opening and knot the thread to finish it.

 4 Fold the four pipecleaners in half. Use one to make antennae and the other three to make pairs of legs. Sew them in place, by sewing over the middle of the fold in each pipecleaner.

5 Glue on small circles of black and white felt to make eyes. Use different coloured circles of felt for spots.

Now your spotty bug is ready to tuck beside your pillow!

10 things to... save animals!

Are you passionate about animals? There are lots of things you can do to make it a safer world for wildlife...

1. Look after nature

You can help protect animals by looking after their habitat (that's their homes!). Don't drop litter or destroy plants when you go out and don't disturb animals if you see any.

2. Clean up!

Volunteer groups help look after beaches or areas of countryside by cleaning up rubbish and repairing damage to the natural habitat. Get your family involved and join a group together!

3. Cut the chemicals

Persuade your parents to use environmentally friendly products around the house - anything from shampoo to floor cleaner. That way, fewer harmful chemicals will go into the waste system and end up in the ground or in the sea.

4. Get in the know

If an animal is endangered it means that it is in danger of dying out. Find out from books or the internet what the most endangered animals are in the world. The more people who know, the more chance they have of being saved!

5. Get inspired

Visit your local national park or zoo and see if you can go on a guided tour. You'll learn lots about animals, why they are in danger and about conservation projects that are happening. You could end up working in animal conservation one day!

6. Write a letter

Write about your favourite endangered animal. Then send your work to your member of parliament and tell them why you think it's important to help endangered animals. Your opinion counts!

7. Join a club

If there's a particular animal that you really like and want to help, such as the tiger, find an organisation that works to protect it. There might be a kids' club that you can join, which will give you up-to-date information and tell you how you can help.

8. Feed the birds

When winter comes, be a bird's best friend and give it extra food to help it survive. You can buy bird seeds and feeders from garden centres or you can make your own. Check the internet for bird feed recipes.

9. Be a bee friend

Bees are having a hard time and their numbers are decreasing. Nobody knows exactly why, but it is thought that everyone can help by planting 'bee friendly' plants in their garden. Ask how at your local garden centre.

10. Conservation project

Next time you do a project or make a presentation to your class, why not make your subject animal conservation? Pick an endangered animal and tell your class about it and what's being done to help save it. Spread the word!

The talent show

The talent show is approaching fast and the girls are in the competition! Unravel Taylor's secret message to find out what she wants to say to her friends!

EW ACN INW HET PECIOMITONT FI EW
YTR ROU RVYE TESB. OG LGISR!

....

....

Hint:
There's no hint
- you should be
good at these
by now!

Jess and the Go Girls

There's just a few weeks to go before the contest for the best young band. Will the Go Girls go for it?

PART 6

Sadie sat down on the edge of Carla's bed. "Look," she began gently, "this is your big chance to perform with your friends. You've all worked so hard."

Carla nodded sadly. "But what about Lucky? He needs me, too."

"I'll look after him for you," Sadie promised. "Every time you're at band practice, I'll make sure he's happy. But he'll still be your dog. He loves you!"

"Will you bring him to the gig?"

"Of course I will!"

Three weeks later, the girls were at a music festival once more. Except this time, they were standing in the wings, waiting to run on stage. Carla's heart was thumping. She was the lead singer in a band! And in the audience were her parents and her big sister – and her little dog! She just hoped that she wouldn't let them down.

"Ready?" Jess squeezed her hand.

"I'm ready!" Carla replied as the loudspeaker boomed "Next on stage – it's THE GO GIRLS!"

The gig was a dream. They blasted through two Star Rock tracks and then launched into their very own song, *Catch a Wave* – and the audience loved it! Then just as Carla opened her mouth to sing out the final words, a tiny black thing flew at her from nowhere! She staggered back into Jess's drum kit and just managed to finish the last note. Lucky had launched himself right into her arms...

Backstage, Carla was downcast. "I'm sorry," she moaned. "I've ruined it by making Sadie bring Lucky to the gig!"

The girls looked glum. Surely there was no chance for them now.

"Ahem," a young man appeared with a clipboard. "Are you Jess? Your band needs to go back on stage – you're the winners!"

"But how can that be?" Jess replied.

"Your act was going really well," the young man explained, "but that trick with the cute dog really sealed it for you. He must be your lucky mascot!"

And so the winning band ran on for the encore – not forgetting Lucky, of course!

The End!

122

Dancing shoes

Taylor loves shoes. Doodle her
dancing shoes here!

Do they
have bows?

Are they
leopard
print?

Are they
silver or
scarlet?

Spot the difference

There are ten tricky differences between these two pictures of the Go Girls performing. Ring them when you've got them!

A

B

Are you a dancing queen?

Read these questions and circle your answers.
Check the panel to find out how many points you scored
and find out if you're a dancing queen!

1 At a party, you always hang out:
A. near the music player
B. near the dance floor
C. near the food

2 Your nickname at school is most likely to be:
A. fabulous feet
B. fancy feet
C. two left feet

3 If a boy asked you to dance, you'd say:
A. No way!
B. I'll show you how!
C. Thanks - that would be fun!

4 One day, you dream about becoming:
A. a choreographer
B. a dance teacher
C. a history teacher

5 Your favourite place to dance would be:
A. at a party with your friends
B. on stage in front of hundreds
C. on TV in front of millions

Add up your points:
1. A = 2 points   B = 3 points   C = 1 point
2. A = 3 points   B = 2 points   C = 1 point
3. A = 1 point   B = 3 points   C = 2 points
4. A = 3 points   B = 2 points   C = 1 point
5. A = 1 point   B = 2 points   C = 3 points

5-8 points
DANCING DISASTER
Dancing's not your best skill, but it's still a lot of fun so who cares if you've got two left feet!

9-11 points
DANCING PRINCESS
You love to dance and you don't mind showing off your moves at a party with your friends!

12-15 points
DANCING QUEEN
You live to dance and you'll take any opportunity to practise your steps – even in the bus queue!

Star maze

The Go Girls are the stars of the show! They receive a big bunch of flowers, but lose it at the festival. Can you find it?

start

end

Puzzle parade

Which two pictures of Taylor are an exact match?

1   2   3   4

When she's not dancing or playing guitar, Taylor keeps herself busy with number puzzles. Can you help her with this one?

Starting at number 8 at the top, hop on one number in each row so that your total is 100 when you reach the last row.

start

8

25	23	28
7	16	40
47	15	34
2	5	31
18	10	3

Taylor's challenge

Take the friendship challenge! Pick your favourite Go Girl and ask your friend to do the same. Match them up on the chart to find the key to your friendship.

	YOUR BEST FRIEND					
	Jess	Roxy	Anna	Milly	Carla	Taylor
Jess	1	2	3	4	5	6
Roxy	2	1	4	5	6	2
Anna	3	4	1	6	2	3
Milly	4	5	6	1	3	4
Carla	5	6	2	3	1	5
Taylor	6	2	3	4	5	1

YOU

WHAT YOUR FRIENDSHIP KEY MEANS...

1 You're so alike, you could be twins!
2 You both love lots of adventure!
3 You like doing the same stuff!
4 You're opposites – but you attract!
5 Your personalities complement each other!
6 You can tell each other your secrets!

Draw Taylor

Copy Taylor's picture into the grid, square by square.

Puzzle parade

Which shadow exactly matches Taylor's necklace?

Taylor's make-up bag has spilled open! Look at this picture closely for 10 seconds, then cover it with your hand. Can you name everything in the picture?

Dancer doodle!

What's your favourite dancing outfit? Doodle it here!

Is it sequins and sparkles?

Is it cool jeans and trainers?

It is a pretty party dress?

Message mix up

Rearrange the strips at the top of the page into the boxes below to reveal Taylor's message to her friends!

| T | I | M | E | . |

| U | S | T | | B |

| A | R | T | S |

| E | | O | N |

| T | H | E | | S |

| Y | O | U | | M |

| S | O | O | N | . |

| H | O | W | | S | T |

Puzzle parade

Fill in the missing letters to spell out six words related to the Go Girls' performance.

S	T	A		E	
	H	Y	T	H	M
V	O	C		L	S
G	R	O		P	
S		N	G	E	R
S		E	P	S	

Now rearrange the missing letters to find an object that Taylor loves. ....

Which of Taylor's friends is hiding in this puzzle picture?

Write her name here:

....

Best friends forever

How well do you know the Go Girls? Use your imagination to fill in the chart. Then add your own information!

	Age	Middle name	Favourite colour
Jess			
Carla			
Anna			
Taylor			
Roxy			
Milly			
Me			

Favourite animal	Favourite hobby	Best talent

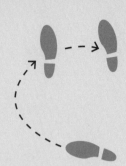

Taylor's dance routine

Taylor is making up some moves for the
Go Girls to use in their act. Look at her list of dance
steps and scribble down your own routine!

DANCE STEPS:

Side step left

Side step right

Spin left

Spin right

Forwards jump

Backwards jump

Hand clap

Turn on the spot

ROUTINE 1:

ROUTINE 2:

ROUTINE 3:

Design Taylor's outfit

Design an outfit for Taylor to wear on stage!

Is she a rock chick?

Is she a pop princess?

Fill it in!

Is YOUR style rock or pop?

....

Design a poster

You're next on stage! Design a poster for a show starring you and your friends!

Puzzle parade

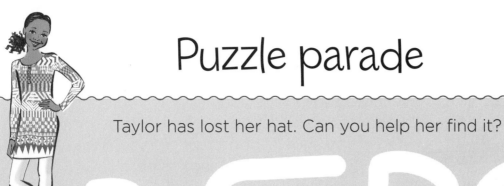

Taylor has lost her hat. Can you help her find it?

Taylor has got cool matching belts for all of the Go Girls.
One doesn't quite match though, can you spot it?

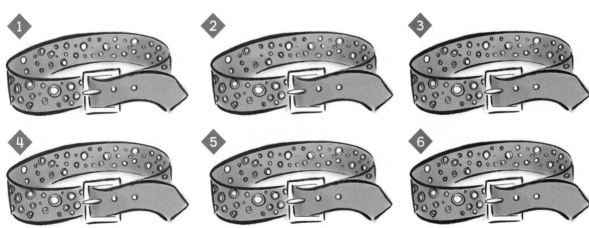

139

Make a scrapbook

A scrapbook helps you keep all your souvenirs in one place so that your memories last for ever! Tickets to shows, photos of friends, notes and cards... put them all here!

You will need

* 6 A4 sheets of thin card
* Hole punch
* 2 A4 sheets of thick card
* Length of thin ribbon
* Felt-tip pens and decorations, such as stickers

1 Punch a hole in the top left-hand corner of 6 sheets of thin card. You can make them all different colours if you like! Make sure the holes are all in the same place and not too close to the edge.

2 Now punch a hole in the two thick pieces of card, again making sure that the holes are in the same place as the other pieces of card.

3 Put all the pieces of card together to make a book. Thread a piece of thin ribbon through the holes, knot securely and tie in pretty bow at the top of the book.

4 Now add a title on the front cover with felt-tip pens and decorate it if you like. You can use stickers, glue on sequins or decorate with glitter glue.

Your scrapbook is ready - so start sticking in your stuff!

My special Scrapbook!

10 things to do... to be on stage!

Have you always fancied being on the stage?
Well, here's a few ideas to get you started!

1. Dance diva?

If you want to be a dancer, the best way to start is to have lessons. But you can also practise on your own. Watch videos of your favourite dancers and see if you can copy what they do!

2. Singer in the making?

Maybe singing is your thing? In that case, sing as much as you can – and maybe get some lessons, too. Join your local choir or sing in a band with your friends. Go for it!

3. Music maestro?

A good way to improve your music skills is to learn to play the piano, the guitar or a percussion instrument. Once you start to learn, you'll find out whether you have an ear for music!

4. Actor for hire?

It doesn't have to be music that puts you on the stage. Perhaps you fancy yourself as a bit of an actor? If that's the case, study your favourite actors and decide what kind of characters might suit you best!

5. Comedy classic?

Always telling jokes? Then maybe you should be a comedian. Write a few funny scripts and try them out on your friends!

6. Work on your look

When performing, you often have to look right as well as sound right. Take a look at yourself in the mirror and decide how you want to look on stage. Don't forget – it can be completely different from your 'normal' look.

7. Enter a talent contest

Your local theatre or festival might run a talent contest. If you're feeling brave, why not enter? It's a good way to practise performing and you might get some feedback to help you improve.

8. School performance

Your school probably has a performance every year – maybe a play or a concert, or even a variety show. Get in touch with the organisers and offer your talents!

9. Behind the scenes

If you love music and theatre but don't want to be in the spotlight, there are plenty of jobs to do behind the scenes. You could help produce the show, paint the scenery or make the costumes.

10. Join a class or a club

If you're serious about being on stage, the best thing to do is join a theatre school, dance club or music class. That way, you'll get lessons and lots of practice in performing. Good luck!

Answers to puzzles

Page 6
The secret message reads: I want to see my favourite band!

Page 8
Pictures 2 and 5 are the same.

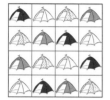

Page 10

Page 12

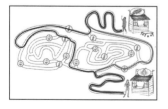

Page 18

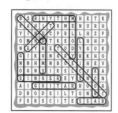

Page 19
From the letters in the word FESTIVALS, you can make: fast, fist, last, late, list, sale, slave, stave, tale, vase, vail, vast, vest, vista.

Picture 3 is the odd one out.

Page 23
£23.80

Flag 6 doesn't have a pair.

Page 25
The secret message reads: Girls, let's go to the juice bar first!

Page 28

Page 30

Page 31
Shadow 3

Pictures 1 and 6

Page 13
Tents 1 and 5 are the same.

There are 47 butterflies.

Page 14
LISTEN TO MUSIC
EAT FOOD
GO CAMPING
MEET FRIENDS
DANCE
HAVE FUN

Pages 16-17

Page 32
Roxy's favourite precious stone is: SAPPHIRE

Page 37

Page 38
Here are a few girls' names beginning with 'R' to start you off: Rachel, Raquel Rebecca, Rhianna, Rosie...

Page 40
Roxy's favourite drink is: JUICE

Page 41
The message is: I am going to star in a rock band.

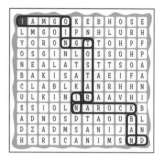

Page 46
Roxy's perfect accessory is the handbag.

These words CAN'T be made out of the letters in the words WINDOW SHOPPING:

SWISH
WISHES
SHOE
NEW
SHINE

Page 49
The secret message reads: Our best skill is knowing how to work as a team.

Page 52

Page 54

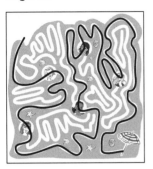

Page 55

Line C

Pictures 3 and 4 match

SURFING is Anna's favourite hobby.

Page 56

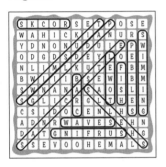

Page 58-59

Page 60

Jess's swimsuit is pink with fish on it.
Roxy's swimsuit is orange with flowers on it.
Anna's swimsuit is blue with waves on it.

Page 61

There are 39 fish.

Anna is 5 minutes late.

Page 65

The words are:
LIFEGUARD
SURFER
ROCK STAR
MANAGER

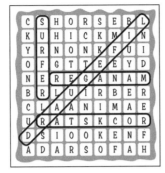

Page 66-67

The most points you can get is 23.

The route is:

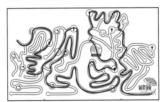

Page 70

Picture 5 is the odd one out.

1. Wax the board
2. Jog to the sea
3. Paddle away from the beach
4. Ride the waves!

Page 73

The secret message reads: My fave picnic food is cupcakes!

Page 76

Page 77

1. True; 2. True; 3. True; 4. False – baguette means a long, thin rectangle shape; 5. True; 6. False – yogurt is made from milk; 7. True; 8. False – olives are fruit that grow on olive trees; 9. True; 10. True; 11. False – a knickerbocker glory is a type of ice-cream sundae; 12. True.

Page 78

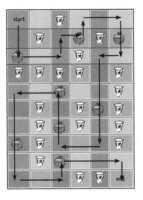

page 80

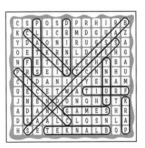

page 84

3	6	2	8	5	7	1	9	4
5	1	7	2	9	4	6	8	3
4	9	8	3	1	6	2	7	5
7	4	6	5	3	8	9	1	2
1	2	5	7	6	9	3	4	8
8	3	9	4	2	1	7	5	6
9	8	1	6	4	3	5	2	7
6	5	4	1	7	2	8	3	9
2	7	3	9	8	5	4	6	1

page 85

Shadow 4

The song titles are:
Best friends forever!
Get ready to go girls!
Dance to the crazy beat!

Page 90

The fake fruits are: Song Berry, Guitarna and Tear Pear.

The word is CHOCOLATE. From the letters in the word CHOCOLATE you can make: chat, colt, cool, hot, latch, late, loot, lot, teach, tool.

Page 91

Jess had sandwiches and sang 2 songs.
Carla had apples and sang 3 songs.
Anna had smoothies and sang 6 songs.
Taylor had cupcakes and sang 5 songs.
Roxy had grapes and sang 4 songs.

Page 92-93

Milly lost her camera.

Page 94

4 and 5 are different.

Milly has the most points, as she has 8.

Page 97

The secret message reads: Playing with puppies is just the best fun

Page 100

Page 102

Page 103

Here are a few girls' names beginning with 'C' to start you off: Candy, Cara, Charlotte, Chelsea, Claudia...

Yes, Carla makes the call on time.

Page 104

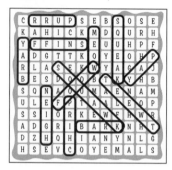

Page 106

Anteater
Bat
Cat
Donkey
Elephant
Firefly
Giraffe
Hamster
Iguana
Jackal
Kiwi
Ladybird
Macaw
Narwhal
Orangutan
Peacock
Quail
Rhinoceros
Shark
Tarantula
Unicorn
Viper
Wallaby
Xolo
Yak
Zebra fish

Page 109

The secret message reads: I am the lead singer. The Go Girls rock!

Page 110

Pictures 2 and 3 are the same.

Picture 2 is the odd one out.

Page 112

From the letters in the word MICROPHONE you can make: come, cone, crone, hero, home, mine, more, morph, nip, on, one, phone, pin, rim, rip.

Shadow 3

Page 113

Carla's favourite creepy crawly is a LADYBIRD

Page 118

SQUEAK
GINGER
HENRY

Picture 3 is the odd one out.

DOG appears in the grid 9 times.

Page 121

The secret message reads: We can win the competition if we try our very best. Go girls!

Page 124

Page 126

Page 127

Pictures 1 and 3 are an exact match.

The route is: 8 + 23 + 7 + 47 +5 + 10 = 100

Page 130

Shadow 3

Page 132

The message reads: You must be on time. The show starts soon.

Page 133

The words are:
STAGE
RHYTHM
VOCALS
GROUP
SINGER
STEPS
Rearrange the missing letters to make the word GUITAR.

Milly is hiding in the picture.

Page 139

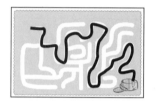

Picture 2 is the odd one out.